SAILING *and* SOARING

The Great Liners and the Great Skyscrapers

WILLIAM H. MILLER

FONTHILL

For Mike and Carol Merwine

dear friends, skyscraper enthusiasts, and creators of superb buildings in miniature

Fonthill Media Limited
Fonthill Media LLC
www.fonthillmedia.com
office@fonthillmedia.com

First published in the United Kingdom and the United States of America 2016

British Library Cataloguing in Publication Data:
A catalogue record for this book is available from the British Library

Copyright © William H. Miller 2016

ISBN 978-1-78155-368-8

The right of William H. Miller to be identified as the author of this work has been asserted by him in accordance with the Copyright, Designs and Patents Act 1988.

Typeset in Minion Pro 11pt on 15pt
Printed and bound by CPI Group (UK) Ltd, Croydon, CR0 4YY

CONTENTS

FOREWORD

In 1906, the rattle of workmen's hammers, the sounds of drills and motors, and the roaring of engines for lifts and cranes filled the air on both sides of the Atlantic. It was the staccato, the 'music' of the Industrial Age, that powerful, pulsating part of the Edwardian world's first decade of the new century. At Clydebank in Scotland and at Newcastle in England, shipyard crews were building the largest liners yet, a pair of near-sisters for the large, very prestigious Cunard Line. These ships, to be named *Lusitania* and *Mauretania*, would measure nearly 800 feet in length; no ship at sea had yet reached that size. At the same time, but some 3,500 miles across the Atlantic, in Lower New York City, the energies of workmen were directed upwards, constructing the 612-foot-tall Singer Building, which would be the tallest skyscraper yet. Both the ships and the building were great symbols of distinction. The public was fascinated by them. It was an age that created a spirited effort—bigger and taller (and also faster) were seen as better. They were also great nationalistic symbols—the might and aptitude of a nation expressed in bolder accomplishment. Great senses of national pride were the finish line, and, adding to the overall excitement, the future was nothing but bright—only larger ships and taller skyscrapers were on the horizon.

First and foremost, I have always loved ocean liners. I collected ephemera from them, sailed aboard them, and have written a long list of books about them. I also give lectures aboard them—talking mostly about bygone passenger ships aboard present-day cruise ships. But I also have a great liking and fascination for skyscrapers, especially those near my home in New York City. Like the great liners, they too are great creations. There is grandeur, might, and special accomplishment in their creation, their being. But there is another similarity: the race for greater size. This parallel has long intrigued me—as bigger liners arrived, taller towers seemed to come into place as well. It has been a very progressive trend throughout the last century or so.

As I am writing this book, Manhattan's World Trade Center—in fact, the tallest office building in the Western Hemisphere—has just opened. At the same time, but southward, in Fort Lauderdale, Florida, the two largest passenger ships yet built, the *Oasis of the Seas* and the *Allure of the Seas*, set sail on weekly voyages to the Caribbean. Interestingly, these two ships are so big, so tall, that they cannot enter New York harbor; they cannot pass under the Verrazano-Narrows Bridge.

As I am writing, it is as exciting today as that period a century ago when the *Lusitania, Mauretania*, and the Singer Building were being created. Today, buildings taller than the World Trade Center in New York are being planned. Similarly, two slightly larger versions of the *Oasis of the Seas* and her twin sister are being built in a French shipyard. So, while the evolution among liners and skyscrapers kept pace over the last hundred or so years, it continues into the foreseeable future. Since New York was the capital of ocean liners for much of the time, I decided to limit my scope to Manhattan skyscrapers.

At the time of writing that excitement continues. Out in Dubai, the 2,717-foot, 162-story-tall Burj Khalifa opened in 2010, and it reigns as the world's tallest skyscraper. In New York, construction crews are adding the finishing touches to 432 Park Avenue, rising above the midtown city at 1,400 feet and ninety-five floors, almost equal in height to the iconic Empire State Building and Manhattan's tallest residential structure yet. Meanwhile, with the international cruise industry booming, a French shipyard is presently constructing the largest passenger ship of all time—the 227,000-ton, 6,500-passenger *Harmony of the Seas*.

Like onlookers back in 1906, I too feel a sense of excitement. This book tells the story of the great liners and the great skyscrapers, past and present.

BILL MILLER
New Jersey, USA
Summer 2015

The great liners and the great skyscrapers—the *Queen Mary* arriving in New York harbor in July 1947, with the Woolworth, Bank of Manhattan, and Cities Services towers in the top background. (*Author's Collection*)

One

RISE IN HEIGHT
The First Great Structures

IN THE 1990s, DURING A summer cruise along the Rhine River, we called in at Cologne. Amidst the cityscape were the soaring twin spires of the local cathedral. At 516 feet, they were once considered as the tallest structures anywhere on earth. Between 1200 and 1870, the tallest structures were in fact Christian churches and cathedrals. Before then, the distinction of tallest structure was in the East. The Lighthouse of Alexandria, completed in about 280 BC, was quite possibly the tallest, but no actual measurement is known. The Great Pyramid at Giza in Egypt was the likely successor, rising to 481 feet, and holding the distinction for an extraordinary 3,800 years.

The title moved to churches and cathedrals in the West in the 1200s when Old Paul's Cathedral in London rose to full height of 489 feet. Within a century, it was surpassed by 524-foot-tall Lincoln Cathedral. By the late nineteenth century, several cathedrals in Europe stood at just under or just over 500 feet. The spire of the Antonelli Edifice in Turin was most likely the tallest by the late nineteenth century, rising 550 feet. The Eiffel Tower, not a building, but a structure, rose to 986 feet in 1889.

The skyscraper emerged in the second half of the nineteenth century. Using iron and steel internal structures (instead of the outer walls) to bear the weight, the 130-foot tall, seven-story Equitable Life Building in New York City was considered the very first skyscraper. The Equitable had an added distinction: it was the tallest building to have elevators. While the title of tallest skyscraper briefly passed to Chicago and even to Milwaukee, New York City had the tallest buildings until 1901 (then with the 390-foot tall Park Row Building). Between 1901 and 1908, the location for world's tallest building shifted to Philadelphia. Capped by a statue of William Penn, the Philadelphia City Hall stood at 548 feet. Paris, with the Eiffel Tower, retained home to the 'world's tallest structure' (and finally surpassed in 1930 by the Griffin Television Tower in Oklahoma). The title of 'world's tallest skyscraper' eventually went back to New York City in 1908, when the 612-foot-tall Singer Building was completed and remained there until the 1,368-foot tall World Trade Center. Consequently, I choose to start my comparison between the great liners and the great skyscrapers with the forty-seven-story Singer Building.

Two

NEEDLE AND THREAD
The Singer Building

I T SEEMED IRONIC THAT ON the very day (22 September 1967) that the *Queen Mary* sailed along the Hudson River on her very last Atlantic voyage, work crews were atop the Singer Building to begin the process of demolition; two icons were passing. But while the *Queen Mary* was given something of a royal sendoff—surrounded by tugs, fireboats, and spectator craft and to a chorus of tooting horns and screeching sirens, the quiet demolition of the Singer went on all but unnoticed. Happily, the *Queen Mary* lives on in gentile retirement as a museum, hotel, and collection of shops out in southern California, at Long Beach; the Singer was, in a matter of months, reduced to scrap and rubble, and gone completely.

The elegant Singer Building was the beginning of taller and taller buildings in New York City and in the United States itself. On the list 100 tallest buildings in the world, ninety-nine of them were located in North America by 1930. Slightly more than half of them were in New York City. A shift to overseas skyscrapers, particularly to Asia, began in 1998, with the Petronas Twin Towers in Kuala Lumpur. In 2015, over sixty of the world's 100 tallest buildings are in Asia. The purpose of these great towers has also changed to far more mixed use—office and residential. In 2015, only four of the world's ten tallest buildings, and twenty-eight of the fifty tallest, are used primarily as offices.

Like a great-grandmother, the Singer Building (or Singer Tower as it was also known) majestically stood at the bottom end of Manhattan Island, rising along lower Broadway at Liberty Street. The forty-seven-story office building was the world's tallest skyscraper for a year, between 1908 and 1909, and also had an added distinction for a time—in 1967, it ranked as the tallest building to be demolished. In 2015, it remained the third tallest building ever to be destroyed (after the World Trade Center towers), but remained the tallest to be purposely demolished by its owner.

The building was commissioned by what was then a household name in American life, the Singer Sewing Machine Company. Singer wanted larger headquarters, but also a stunning example of its success and its place in the American corporate community. The company's previous headquarters were farther north, at 561 Broadway, between Prince and Spring Streets. Still part of the Soho district, this structure was dubbed the 'Little Singer Building' after the new tower was completed.

Singer hired architect Ernest Flagg, an exponent of Beaux-Arts architectural style, to design the new building. He was actually an old friend, having designed the earlier Singer Building. Singer wanted a tall, statuesque building, while Flagg himself believed that buildings taller than ten and fifteen floors should be set back, occupying as little as a quarter of the lot. It was capped by a flag pole affixed to its tower, which would be removed in the 1940s. When brand new, the Singer had surpassed the nearby Park Row Building, completed in 1899 and which stood at twenty-nine floors and 391 feet; the Singer was over 200 feet taller and nearly twenty floors higher.

From left to right:

The rattle of hammers—construction of the Singer Building in 1906. (*Albert Wilhelmi Collection*)

Ever gracious, the Singer Building towers above an early Lower Manhattan skyline. (*South Street Seaport Museum*)

Early skyscraper: the legendary Flatiron Building on 23rd Street. (*South Street Seaport Museum*)

Bird's-Eye View of Lower New York.

The Singer Building was an immediate success, winning high praises; it featured an observation deck, which was exceptionally popular in the early years, but as the building's height was surpassed, and with dwindling attendance, it was closed in the 1930s. Architectural historian and skyscraper enthusiast Albert Wilhelmi recalled:

The Singer Building in 1909 was an engineering marvel and the equivalent of the *Lusitania* and *Mauretania*. They were the tallest and longest in the world. And their design was very similar—they were very elegant.

Even as late as 2005, thirty-eight years after it was demolished, *New York Times* architectural critic Christopher Gray took to giving the Singer Building high praise:

The lobby had the quality of 'celestial radiance' seen in world's fair and exposition architecture of the period. A forest of marble columns rose high to a series of multiple small domes of delicate plasterwork, and Flagg [the architect] trimmed the columns with bronze beading. A series of large bronze medallions placed at the top of the columns were alternately rendered in the monogram of the Singer Company and, quite inventively, as a huge needle, thread and bobbin.

Above left: The grand main lobby of the forty-seven-floor Singer Building. (*Albert Wilhelmi Collection*)

Above right: Another lobby view. The letter 'S' is mounted at the top of each column. (*Albert Wilhelmi Collection*)

Opposite page:

A postcard of Lower Manhattan dated 1914, with the Woolworth and Singer buildings to the top left. (*Albert Wihelmi Collection*)

Albert Wilhelmi recalled:

I loved the Singer Building since I was a boy of fifteen. I used to visit an old bookshop in my hometown of Philadelphia and often found books about New York City and, in particular, its buildings. I would buy them. The Singer Building was always featured. It became the building of my dreams. Even to this day, it remains one of my favorites, one of the most interesting of all skyscrapers. Also, at my doctor's office, there was a framed picture hanging on the wall of the Manhattan skyline. It was an old photo with the Singer Building as the tallest of what was to me the magical Lower Manhattan skyline. Designed by Ernest Flagg, a discipline of the Beaux Arts style as well as the French Nouveau style, he was also a modernist. Consequently, the Singer Building was quite modern for its time. The center of the Tower was practically all glass. It was very modern for its time and also was set back from the street. It stood by itself. The City Investment Building was just next door to the Singer. A huge building, it practically surrounded the Singer. For the future, Flagg was a champion of changing the zoning codes.

By the 1930s, the Singer—while still noticeable and even eye-catching—was dwarfed by what the late architect-designer Ted Conrad called 'Lower Manhattan's big five'. The dome-topped Singer was surrounded by the Cities Service, Bank of Manhattan, Woolworth, City Bank Farmers Trust, and Irving Trust towers, each of them taller and with four of them being Art Deco slender.

With the construction of the likes of the Chase Manhattan Bank Building in 1960 and, later in the same decade, the coming of the likes of the exceptional World Trade Center, the Singer seemed more and more like, as Ted Conrad called it, 'some very old maiden aunt'. He added:

It might have been nice and certainly sentimental to keep it around for years to come, to bring smiles to the faces of architectural preservationists, but the time was not right. Older skyscrapers were not then being converted to luxury apartments or hotels. The Singer had outlived its usefulness.

The Singer Company sold the tower in 1961 and moved its headquarters uptown, to Rockefeller Center. In fact, the age of the wide use of the sewing machine was already in its slow decline. William Zeckendorf, a Manhattan real estate baron, had hoped that the New York Stock Exchange would move its headquarters into the Singer Building. The idea never materialized and, while many floors were empty, mighty United States Steel bought the tower in 1964 (along with the adjacent City Investment Building), but purposely for demolition. The Singer would be replaced by the US Steel Building. Unfortunately, the Singer did not have official landmark designation. If it was a landmark, it might have been saved and perhaps sold to different owners and put to continuing use. According to the late Der Scutt, a noted New York City architect who has 1 Astor Place and the Trump Tower among his credits:

…the building was no longer practical: the infrastructure, the plumbing and electricity, were in need of complete change and renewal, it needed a complete air-conditioning system and, possibly most of all, small upper-floor, interior spaces. Demolition was inevitable. The Woolworth and even some of those tall Wall Street towers might also have been in danger. They were no long economically practical.

Using a single crane, the Singer was steadily reduced to a steel frame, in the fall and winter of 1967–68. 'The smile of Lower of Manhattan seemed to be missing a tooth, a front tooth at that,' added Ted Conrad.

Singer Building, New York.

Above: A postcard of the regal-looking Singer Building.
(*Albert Wilhelmi Collection*)

Right: Looking north to the Singer Building, 1912.
(*Der Scutt Collection*)

Beginning in the late 1920s, skyscrapers would rapidly increase in size. Plans were laid, construction began, and boom times seemed to be the tone of the future. At least four towers of fifty stories and higher were planned for Lower Manhattan. Here is the fifty-seven-floor City Bank Farmers Trust Company building, completed in 1931. (*Port Authority of New York and New Jersey*)

Clockwise from above left:

An aerial view of Lower Manhattan towers—the Singer Building is on the far left. (*ALF Collection*)

A poetic winter's afternoon view looking south along the East River—the Brooklyn Bridge dominates, with the silhouetted Singer Building to the right. (*Der Scutt Collection*)

The evolution over the ages of tall structures. (*Albert Wilhelmi Collection*)

Seen from the top deck of a shuttling, trans-Hudson ferry, the Singer Building dominates the Lower Manhattan skyline. This view dates from 1907. (*Albert Wilhelmi Collection*)

Three

BRITISH TRIUMPH ON THE SEAS
The Lusitania and Mauretania

IT WAS THE BEGINNING OF a rather long list of royal and near-royal launchings for the great Cunard Steam-Ship Company Limited (as it was long-known). Her Grace the Duchess of Roxburge did the honors for the launching of the *Mauretania* at Newcastle in September 1906. It was all quite noteworthy and newsworthy; ocean liners had been proclaimed, after all, 'the greatest moving objects yet made by man'.

The British were deeply concerned after the turn of the century by the rising dominance and soaring popularity of the big German four-stackers on the prestigious North Atlantic run. It was not just about Cunard and their position, but also about national pride and prestige and standing. Ministers in London were worried further, even aggravated when the nation's second largest liner firm, the White Star Line, was sold to multi-millionaire J. P. Morgan's empire in America. Even if White Star ships would continue to fly the British flag, they were still American-owned. A salvage plan of sorts was devised. The government turned to the Cunard Line, then having the biggest fleet on the Atlantic, and offered large, liberal loans to build not one, but two express liners. They would be the largest ships in the world as well as the fastest. And the pie was sweetened. hefty operating sub sidies were included. They were also to represent, especially to the rival Germans and the all-important Americans, the best of British technology, engineering, and overall design. In fact, they were to be great symbols of Britain's supremacy in marine propulsion.

The selection of propulsion machinery for these new 'super Cunarders' followed a very interesting and very successful experiment with the then-new steam turbine system aboard another, but smaller Cunarder, the *Carmania*, commissioned in 1905. The efficiency of the steam turbines aboard that 20,000-ton ship was in fact quite startling. It was quite clearly the beginning of the more efficient and powerful steam-turbine-powered ocean liner.

The new twins followed the Cunard naming practice of using Roman geographic locations. The first of the pair, the 31,500-ton *Lusitania*, was named for Roman Portugal; the *Mauretania* took her name from Roman Morocco. They were statistically impressive as well, being some 10,000 tons larger than the largest German four-stacker. These were also given four funnels, but were evenly spaced, creating, to many, a finer appearance. Almost everything about them was newsworthy, often mind-boggling; their funnels, painted in Cunard's orange-red and black, dominated the waterfront at Liverpool and even New York. Below decks, there were twenty-five boilers and 192 furnaces aboard each ship. There was a storage capacity for 6,000 tons of coal, which produced a great service speed of 24–25 knots, which meant a consumption of 1,000 tons of coal per day.

The *Lusitania*—which had a capacity for 2,165 passengers—was commissioned in September 1907; the *Mauretania* in the following November. After the quadruple screw *Lusitania* captured the Blue Riband with the first average speed greater than 25 knots in 1907,

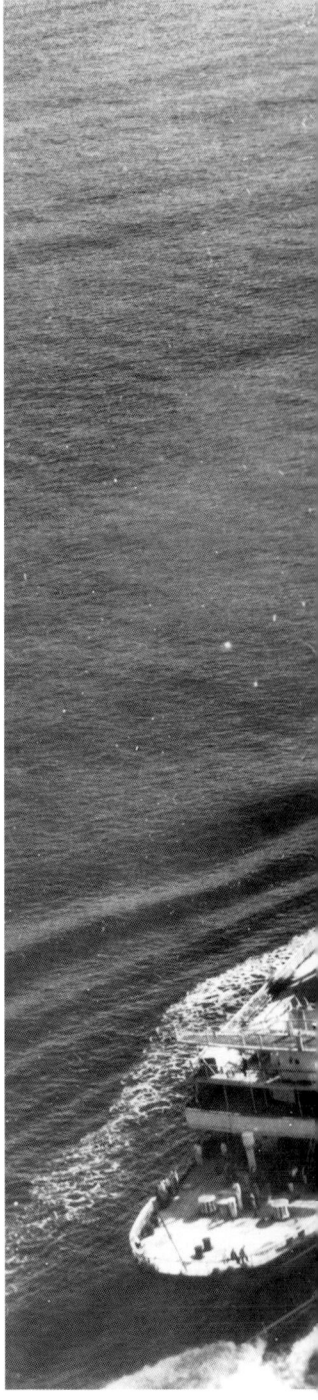

Far left: Cunard's splendid *Mauretania* during her sea trials. The 790-foot-long liner went on to become one of the most successful, popular, and beloved liners of all time. (*Cronican-Arroyo Collection*)

Middle: An aerial view of the brilliant *Mauretania,* which made six-day passages between Liverpool and New York at a speed of 25 knots (*Cronican Arroyo Collection*)

Above: Shipboard luxury, the two-deck high well of the first-class dining salon aboard the *Mauretania.* (*Author's Collection*)

Below: Easy links between shore-side railways and the arrivals and departures of the great liners were part of the travel experience and convenience. (*Author's Collection*)

her maiden year, Britain very proudly retained Atlantic speed honors for well over two decades. Soon after the *Lusitania*'s triumph, the *Mauretania* made an even faster run, above 26 knots, and eventually established herself as the faster of the pair and holder of the coveted Blue Riband. For this great distinction, lasting for twenty-two years until 1929, more travelers preferred the *Mauretania*. The British government and Cunard were especially proud of these speedy sister-ships and more specifically of the legendary *Mauretania*, surely one of the most successful and well-liked liners ever to sail.

The interiors of these newest of Cunarders represented the glories of British and European design and décor. The decorative themes ranged from French Renaissance to English country, and included grand lounges, elegant smoking rooms, libraries, salons, private parlors, and even exceptional Edwardian palm courts. All of the bathroom fixtures in first class were silver plated and the *Mauretania* had an added feature—the first hydraulically-operated barber's chair ever to go to sea.

But if the first class and second class had the greatest comfort, luxuries, even added notations, Cunard made its greatest profits in Spartan third class and steerage. As the latest of the 'floating palaces,' the *Lusitania* and *Mauretania* were no exceptions. Onboard the 790-foot-long *Mauretania*, her accommodations were divided between 560 in first class, 475 second class, and a huge 1,300 down in third class.

Between 1900 and 1915, 12.5 million immigrants crossed the Atlantic to the New World. In 1907, at its peak, there were 1.2 million immigrants and nearly 90 percent of them made the journey, from six days to as long as three weeks, in third class or steerage; 1 million immigrants came from Britain alone. They lived in crowded, sometimes poorly ventilated, lower deck quarters, often in dormitories. Usually, they were only allowed out on the open decks for an hour each day.

At New York, third class and steerage passengers were unloaded from passenger ships that were anchored in the lower reaches of the

Above: In her final years (1933–35), the splendid *Mauretania* was painted all-white and sent off on tropical cruises. In the background, the Lower Manhattan skyline includes the Woolworth Building (left), the Singer Building (center), and the Cities Services and Bank of Manhattan buildings (right). (*Cunard*)

Left: The ship's Palladian Lounge was one of the grandest spaces onboard. The decorative theme was ivory walls and rose brocade with touches of mahogany and Chinese lacquer. (*Norman Knebel Collection*)

Life on the liners—bellboys enjoy some fun.
(*Cunard*)

harbor known as The Narrows. These immigrant passengers were taken by tenders, ferries, and even barges to Ellis Island, the US government inspection station situated just north of the Statue of Liberty. Only the first and second class passengers were permitted to remain and proceed to the Manhattan or Hoboken docks.

Sea life in general, especially in first class, had its rituals. Passengers loved to sit in large, lavish lounges and especially around fireplaces, which were considered a high point in elegance on the great liners. They were usually entirely artificial, of course, having electrically lighted logs. Great, domed skylights were also a fascination point and flooded lounges and salons with great quantities of daylight. These settings were often onboard refuges from the furies and pounding of huge Atlantic seas, and more especially those ferocious winter storms. Other public rooms, including the writing and card rooms and wood-paneled libraries, were also popular havens of shipboard life. Dining in first class was, of course, often quite exceptional; for example, onboard the *Mauretania* it was a two-deck affair with tables on both levels. One Cunard brochure noted, 'When the

ship is in evening dress, the dining room is as gay and brilliant as the Armenonville in Paris or as socially correct as the Berkeley in London.' The dining room onboard the *Mauretania* included the captain's table in the middle and with a monster arrangement of palms and long-stemmed greens rising up into the balcony area. The center portion under the dome was kept free of tables and was used for dancing during the dinner hour.

Crewmembers aboard the great liners were, in many ways, a unique breed for seamen. For example, to be employed on a Cunard passenger liner was considered prestigious in itself. Often, special contacts were needed just for employment. One captain later recalled, 'The officers in particular were career men, often with over forty or fifty years of service and all with the same shipping line.'

Hideously, the *Lusitania* was sunk by a German U-boat while sailing off Ireland on 7 May 1915; there were 1,198 casualties. The *Mauretania* was far more fortunate, sailing on for twenty-seven years before being scrapped in 1935.

Four

'THE LIGHT THAT NEVER FAILS'
The Metropolitan Life Tower

Beginning back in the 1950s, I often watched the great liners come and go from my favorite perch along the Hudson, in my hometown of Hoboken, and I also studied the city skyline; it was fascinating. Daytime views were expectedly intriguing, but nighttime had its own unique fascination—seeing the lighted towers. One of the more interesting was the Metropolitan Life Tower, located on East 23rd Street in Manhattan and all but directly due east of Hoboken. Tall and slender, the building had a well-lighted clock on four sides while on the very top there was a single white light—'the light that never fails,' according to the building's owners, the Metropolitan Life Insurance Company. On the hour, however, the white light briefly switched off, changed to red and then the red flashed equal to the hour. It was like some unique time piece.

When Metropolitan Life decided on new headquarters capped by a tall tower in 1905, they looked farther uptown, away from the 'clutter' of Lower Manhattan, to a site at East 23rd Street and Madison Avenue. The actual address was also distinctive; 1 Madison Avenue. They wanted an individualistic building, a classical landmark, and, with the architectural firm of Napoleon LeBrun & Sons, the tower was stylized after the great and grand structure of the Campanile in Venice. 'After the Campanile in Venice had collapsed, the Metropolitan Life Tower was a replica in many ways, but also twice the size,' noted Albert Wilhelmi. 'The Tower was a supersized Campanile.'

The fifty-two-floor tower, which would be the world's tallest skyscraper for almost four years, from 1909 until 1913, was actually an addition to lower Metropolitan Life Home Office Building, dubbed the 'East Wing,' constructed along Madison Avenue in 1893. That building was replaced in 1953–57, leaving the tower with changed surroundings. However, the 700-foot-tall tower has changed itself; it was modernized in an extensive progress between 1960 and 1964, and again in 1998. Originally sheathed in Tuckahoe marble, the tower's exteriors were recovered in plain limestone during the renovations and modernization work of the early 1960s. When finished, the entire building seemed more contemporary, even sleek. The original Renaissance Revival details were removed along with much of the building's early period ornamentation.

A great symbol when looking along 23rd Street, the tower was distinctive not only by its tower and richly gilded top, but by the four clock faces on each side. Located between the twenty-fifth and twenty-seventh floors, each clock is 26½ feet in diameter and each number 4 foot tall. Each minute hand weighs half a ton.

By the late 1920s, Metropolitan Life began to outgrow its headquarter tower and building below and so planned for additional space in the form of record-breaking building; 100 floors in total and positioned just north between East 24th and 25th streets. Noted architect Harvey Wiley Corbett left his position on the design team (then planning what would become Rockefeller Center) in 1928 and made

Above: Looking south along Madison Avenue, the fifty-two-story Metropolitan Life Building was under construction from 1908–09. (*ALF Collection*)

Right: A postcard of the newly completed Metropolitan Life Insurance Building. (*Albert Wilhelmi Collection*)

Inset: An evocative impression of the building on a summer's evening. (*Author's Collection*)

initial plans for what then would be the tallest building in the world. The Wall Street Crash in October 1929 changed things, however. Ideas for the tower were scrapped. Only the thirty-two-floor base would be built, which was finally completed in 1950. Named the Metropolitan Life North Building, it is today known as Eleven Madison Avenue and its primary tenant is a Swiss bank.

By the 1980s, the upper tower was bathed extensively in a yellow, almost golden, light. The Metropolitan Life Tower became even more of a jewel in the city's nighttime skyline. Nearby, the New York Life Building was now lighted as well. Together, they created an exquisite pair.

The tower had another refurbishing and modernization in an extended, three-year project from 1999 to 2002. The building was covered in scaffolding for months. In the multi-million dollar process, a new, computerized, multicolored nighttime lighting system was added to the upper floors and tower—this system was later used on the Empire State Building. The colors changed to denote particular holidays and special occasions. By midnight, the lighting was usually switched-off. The cupola at the very top—the original 'eternal light' of the Metropolitan Life Company—remained lit, however.

Just south of the Metropolitan Life Building, a sixty-story apartment tower was created in 2009. It also created a visual contrast in architectural design over 100 years. (*Author's Collection*)

Looking south-east over Pennsylvania Station in this 1939 view, the Metropolitan Life Building is almost in top-center with 'the light that never fails'. (*Der Scutt Collection*)

Above left: With a slight haze, the New York Life Building (left) and the Metropolitan Life Building seem to complement one another. New York Life was constructed in 1928, almost twenty years after Metropolitan Life. (*ALF Collection*)

Above right: Looking south from the top of the Empire State Building in 2010, the Metropolitan Life Building has retained its elegance and style after a century. (*Albert Wilhelmi Collection*)

In glowing white light, it remained a tribute to the 106-year-old building's glorious past and 'the light that never fails.'

Of course, time would make the buildings, and especially the tower, less efficient and less practical. Metropolitan Life finally discontinued using the tower as its world headquarters in 2005, and a string of ownerships and ideas for reuse followed. Quite quickly, the building was sold—first to SL Green Realty Corporation, who planned to convert it to luxury apartments, and then, in 2007, to Africa Israel Investments. Including the lower building, the tower changed hands for $200 million. Few changes and little other work was done, however. Designer Tommy Hilfiger and a partner planned to buy the building in 2011 (for $170 million) for conversion, once again, to luxury condominiums. Hilfiger soon withdrew and then Africa Israel sold the tower to Marriott International in January 2012. After undergoing extensive, very thorough renovations in 2013–14, the tower was restyled as the New York Edition Hotel. Edition Hotels, with properties in London and Miami as well, was sold (in early 2013 for $815 million) to Middle Eastern buyers, the Abu Dhabi Investment Authority. Marriott continued as hotel managers, however. The Edition Hotel reopened in 2015.

When it opened in 1909, the 700-foot-tall Metropolitan Life Tower was the world's tallest building. Over a century later, it was no longer even included in a listing of world's tallest 300 skyscrapers. Times and indeed skyscrapers had changed—and grown as well.

Overlooking Madison Square Park with the Flatiron Building in the distance. (*Albert Wilhelmi Collection*)

Five

AN IMPOSING TRIO
Olympic, Titanic, and Britannic

O N A WARM SPRING EVENING in 2010, I was guest speaker at the annual convention of the Titanic International Society. Several hundred devotees of the tragic White Star Line—horrifically sunk on her maiden voyage, no less—and, to some extent, other noted liners, had gathered up in Needham, Massachusetts. Conveniently, Boston was close by. I gave a talk on the great Atlantic liners of the twentieth century. I was hardly an expert on the *Titanic* and her demise and all the details in the aftermath, and so sensibly, I imagined, kept my talk to an overview—from the *Mauretania* through to the modern age of the *Queen Mary 2* and super-mega cruise ships like the $1.5 billion, 6,400-bed *Oasis of the Seas.*

Indeed, we had progressed and grown and, alas, the race for bigger and better was still on. The 882-foot-long *Titanic* was the biggest of her day, in 1912, when in that spring she steamed out of the Harland & Wolff shipyard at Belfast in Northern Ireland. She made course for Southampton, to make preparations for her maiden westbound crossing to New York. All eyes were focused on this newest of the Atlantic's floating palaces. She was the biggest, at least for the time being, but had a very unique, added cache; she was said to be the world's first unsinkable ship. Quite simply, she was unique. She was height of that Industrial Age spirit—bigger, better, yet more notable and distinctive.

That race was the biggest, longest, and of course the fastest, and certainly prevailed in shipping company board rooms and design offices. Cunard's *Lusitania* and *Mauretania* were the world's largest liners in 1907, coming in at just under 33,000 tons and stretching 790 feet in length. The company's arch rival, White Star Line—owned by American tycoon J. P. Morgan but still flying British colors—took up the challenge, seeking to attract more passengers. They were especially interested in increasing the numbers traveling in top-deck first class; linking it all to safety, lower-deck emigrants in Spartan steerage might also be suitably impressed and then lured to book passage as well. White Star planned three ships overall—the first two as a pair, the 45,324-gross-ton, 882-foot-long *Olympic* and then the *Titanic.* Slightly bigger still, the 48,158-ton *Gigantic* would follow. White Star's place in the hierarchy of Atlantic liner travel seemed assured, at least for the time being. At the same time, Cunard had their splendid 45,000-ton *Aquitania* on the drawing boards, but far more significantly, the Germans, in the form of the Hamburg-America Line, were making their first drawings for a colossal threesome—ships that would become the 52,000-ton *Imperator*, then the 54,000-ton *Vaterland* and, finally, the 56,000-ton *Bismarck.* The ocean-liner race had begun.

Business was booming as the first decade of the twentieth century was drawing to a close. By 1910, with ships growing larger as well as more luxurious, the White Star Line, with no ambition toward great speed or Blue Riband records, decided to concentrate on greater size and grander accommodations. Their three new liners would be the largest afloat. Internally, they would be the most splendid liners of

R.M.S.

TITANIC

White Star Line
1912

A splendid cutaway view of the immortal *Titanic* by noted artist Ken Marschall. (*Ken Marschall Collection*)

their day on the Atlantic, each with an Arabian indoor pool (the first ever on an Atlantic liner), first-class staterooms decorated in eleven different schemes, and a palm court of lush greenery.

The first of the trio, the *Olympic*, was launched at Harland & Wolff shipyard at Belfast, in Northern Ireland, on 20 October 1910. But White Star's greatest and perhaps proudest day came six months later, on 31 May, when the second big liner, the *Titanic*, was launched at noon. Then, in the afternoon, invited guests, the dignitaries, friends of the line, and of course the press, boarded the completed, 2,764-passenger *Olympic* for her very first run, an overnight delivery voyage to Southampton. Along with her great size, the innards of the sparkling new *Olympic* were her most attractive feature. To the excited, much-interested press, she was dubbed the greatest of the 'floating palaces'. White Star Line was pleased and honored, and

look forward to the second ship, which was slightly larger, at 46,300 tons. Again, a British-flag liner would be the world's largest and, to many, the most splendid.

As with second sister ships, White Star publicists worked especially hard to find a special identity for the 21-knot, triple-screw *Titanic*. Their efforts were quite thorough—she was already a well-known ship even before her maiden sailing. The company actually went a step further by calling her 'the world's first unsinkable ship.' She had been fitted with extra watertight compartments and, because of White Star's absolute confidence, there were too few lifeboats and lifesaving gear for her maximum 2,600 passengers and 900 crew.

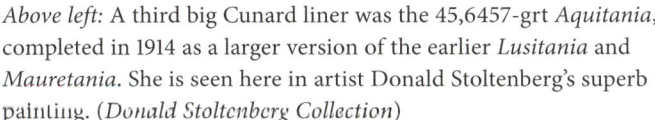

Above left: A third big Cunard liner was the 45,6457-grt *Aquitania*, completed in 1914 as a larger version of the earlier *Lusitania* and *Mauretania*. She is seen here in artist Donald Stoltenberg's superb painting. (*Donald Stoltenberg Collection*)

Above right: The elegant Louis XVI restaurant in first class aboard the 901-foot-long *Aquitania*. (*Norman Knebel Collection*)

Right: The 882-foot-long *Olympic* completed at the Harland & Wolff shipyard in Belfast, Northern Ireland, in a photo from 1911. (*Author's Collection*)

The 2,764-passenger *Olympic* had a comparatively long and successful career—she was in service from 1911 until 1935. (*Richard Faber Collection*)

But the gild on White Star's golden rose began to tarnish and rather quickly. The flag-waving, horn-honking, and festive atmosphere of the *Titanic*'s maiden voyage from Southampton (via Cherbourg and Queenstown) to New York began on 10 April 1912. There were, it seems, some unlucky omens even as the ship set off from British shores. At Southampton, while undocking, she nearly collided with the American liner *New York*. But far greater trouble was ahead. The great tragedy of that westward maiden crossing is extremely well-documented—in hundreds of books, over 300 poems, and seventy-five songs. It has been the subject of a Broadway musical and Hollywood's first $1 billion mega-film by James Cameron. Fascination with the *Titanic* and her sinking seems unending. Suffice it to say that, on the night of the 14th, she sideswiped with an iceberg that ripped a 300-foot-long gash in her starboard side. The cut was fatal; the ship doomed. Two-and-a-half hours later, she sank in a position 380 miles east of Newfoundland and in 12,000 feet of freezing North Atlantic water. An estimated 1,522 passengers and crew perished. Less than two hours later, the first rescue ship appeared, Cunard's little *Carpathia*, and began taking-on the 705 survivors (or some 32 percent of those who had sailed on the *Titanic*).

The tragedy was the worst sea disaster to date and from which the White Star never fully recovered. Safety aboard passenger ships was improved thereafter. To some, the disaster was so shattering, so demoralizing, and so dramatic that it was looked upon as the beginning of the end of the British Empire. Dr Jay Wolff, an historian and port lecturer on modern-day cruise ships, gives a very insightful talk on the *Titanic* disaster:

It was an end to the age of innocence, that age of optimism.... The sinking of the greatest ship yet built and one that was unsinkable, which in itself was pure and outright defiance, was a great turning point. And it was all cemented just two years later when World War I started and the entire world changed forever. Sadly, we have never regained that innocence that unbridled optimism, which ended with the sinking of the *Titanic*.

The third of the White Star trio was, in ways, as unfortunate as the *Titanic*. She lasted a year, having never even had a commercial maiden voyage to New York. Largest of all, she was intended to be named *Gigantic*. However, on the heels of the *Titanic* disaster, a name reflecting grandiose size seemed unwise. Instead, the name *Britannic* was selected. Launched in February 1914, her completion was halted when the war broke out that August. In November 1915, the British Admiralty ordered that the 2,573-berth ship be completed, but as a hospital ship. A year later, on 21 November 1916, and while on duty in the Aegean Sea, she ran into a German-laid mine, exploded and then sank with the loss of twenty-one lives. Sadly, the *Britannic* was one of the least-known big liners of her time and one of the least fortunate of the floating palaces.

In September 2004, *The New Yorker* magazine ran a feature article on sea disasters. The cover art included the *Titanic* and the Empire State Building. (*The New Yorker* magazine)

Six

FIVE AND DIME STORES
The Woolworth Building

On a winter's night in 2013, I was fortunate to be among a specially invited, celebratory group of over 100 to have a guided tour of the illustrious Woolworth Building and to attend a birthday reception afterwards; it was the iconic building's 100th birthday. The highly detailed knowledge of the building's resident architect and chief engineer was equaled only by his great love and high regard for the building. He was our fascinating guide. We toured the glorious lobby, visited some upper floors, and went down to the vast basements (with its huge furnaces and boilers, former coal bunkers, and the long closed, boarded-up indoor swimming pool). Afterward, on a middle floor (but not the very top, which was already undergoing reconstruction and renovations), we toasted the building's centenary with champagne and cake. Quite restricted for security reasons in recent years, we were quite fortunate to be in this extraordinary structure.

Frank Woolworth had great success with his five-and-dime stores and by 1909–10 looked to build a larger, more splendid headquarters. He and his real estate agents looked to Lower Manhattan and, by the winter of 1911, found a suitable site at 233 Broadway, which Woolworth purchased for $4.5 million.

Woolworth hired Cass Gilbert and wanted a neo-Gothic building, one originally planned to be 420 feet in height and with twenty floors. However, ideas soon changed; it became 792 feet in height, with sixty floors and as many as 5,000 windows. The Woolworth Tower would be the tallest building in the world, surpassing the Metropolitan Life Tower by almost 100 feet. The structure cost $13.5 million and quickly became a symbol not only of Woolworth, but of New York City. It could be seen for miles around on a clear day.

Albert Wilhelmi noted:

There is that charming story of Frank Woolworth asking Metropolitan Life Insurance Company for a loan to build his new tower, but for some reason, Metropolitan Life turned down Woolworth. Woolworth then decided to make his new building taller than the Metropolitan Life Tower. Woolworth wanted the tallest building the world. He also wanted a very elegant building and so looked to the Parliament buildings in London for further inspiration. Indeed, the Woolworth was the tallest for some years and very elegant. It was similar, being built in the same era, as the next generation of world's largest liners, the *Olympic* and *Titanic* of the White Star Line, the *Imperator* and *Vaterland* of the Hamburg America Line and the *Aquitania* of Cunard.

President Woodrow Wilson officially opened the building on 24 April 1913, by switching-on a nighttime cascade of white lights. The President remained in Washington, however, and used a switch from his office in the White House. The Woolworth Tower was open for business. F. W. Woolworth Company occupied only one-and-a-half floors at the start, renting the other floors for income.

Municipal and Woolworth Bldgs., New York.

Above left: The newly completed Woolworth Building stands tall over the bottom end of the Hudson River. (*Albert Wilhelmi Collection*)

Above right: A view of the grand Woolworth lobby. (*Albert Wilhelmi Collection*)

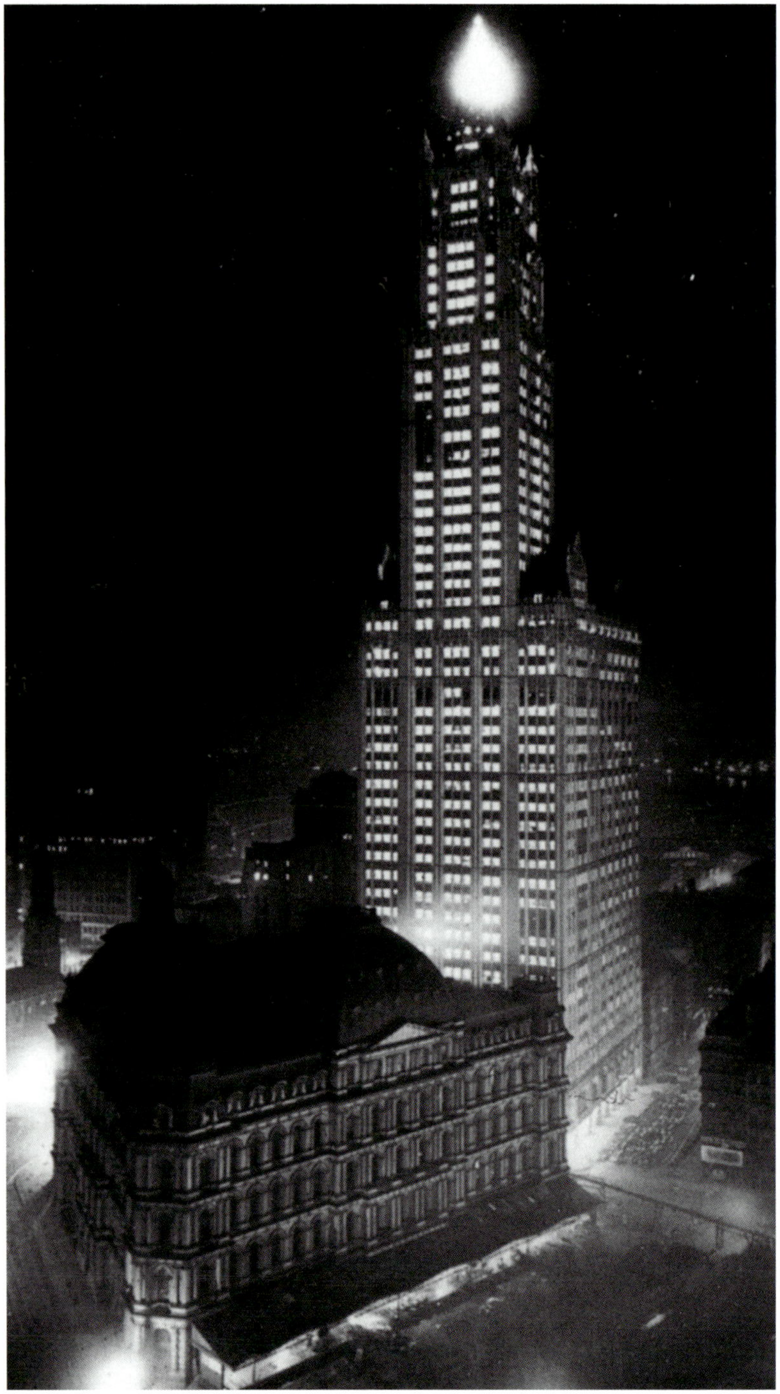

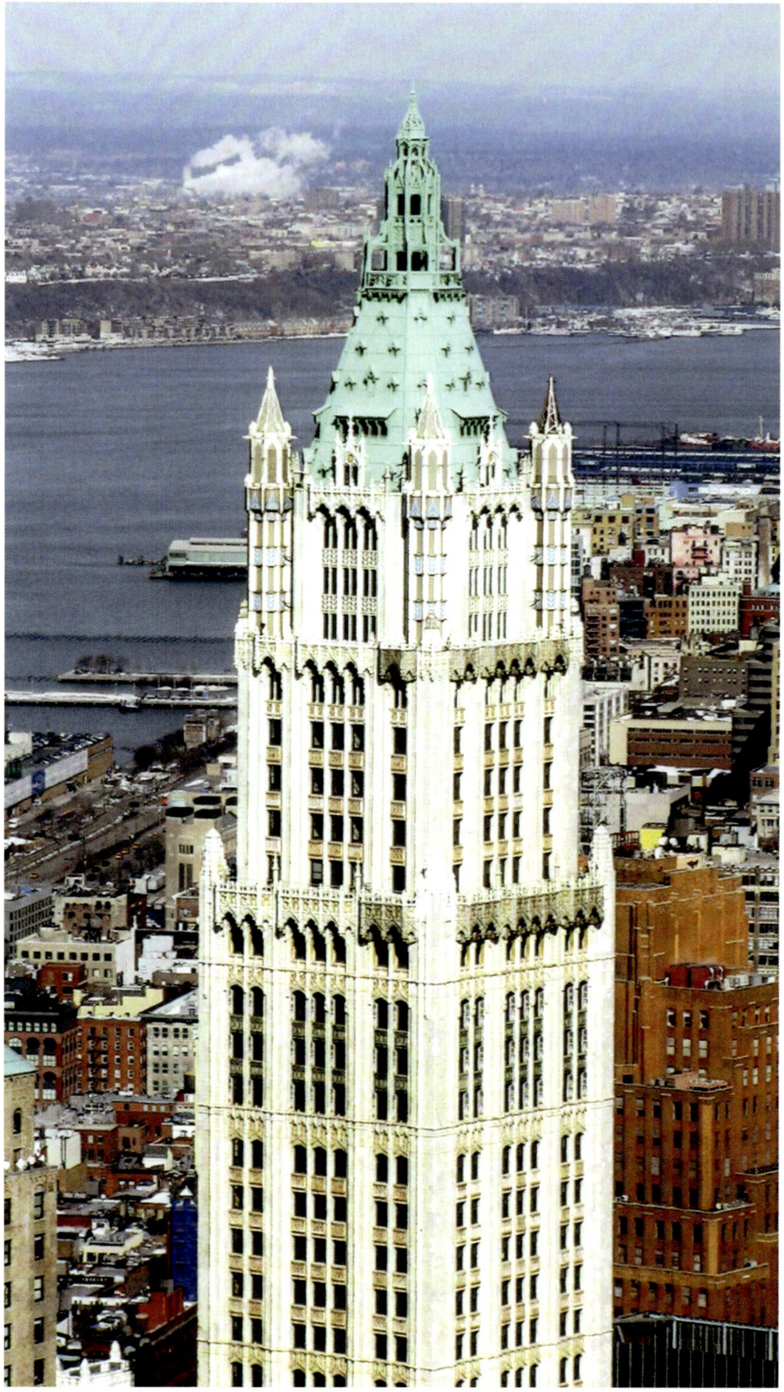

Above: A vast aerial of Lower Manhattan in 1925—the 792-foot-tall Woolworth Building is to the far right; the 919-foot-long *Berengaria* is heading down the Hudson River. (*Cunard*)

Right: Reading 'Above the clouds,' a ticket to the top of the Woolworth Building. (*Albert Wilhelmi Collection*)

Opposite page:

Left: Festivity: Opening day in 1913 for the 792-foot-tall Woolworth Building. (*ALF Collection*)

Right: Looking north from the sixty-sixth floor top of the Deco-styled former Cities Services Building, the Woolworth retains its great elegance and high style in this view taken on a cold winter's morning in 2012. (*Albert Wilhelmi Collection*)

Columbia Records was one of the very first tenants, and installed a recording studio on one floor and, in 1917, recorded the likes of the Original Dixieland Jazz Band there. The Woolworth was also fitted with high-speed elevators, which increased the office-to-elevator process and which appealed to many renters. In the 1920s, the Woolworth Building was completely full of tenants.

At the start, the Woolworth and the Singer building, located just a few city blocks to the south, dominated the Lower Manhattan skyline. The Metropolitan Life Tower stood almost alone farther uptown, along East 23rd Street. The three buildings all but reigned supreme as tallest and symbols of might and success until the first of the Art Deco towers began to sprout upwards in the late 1920s. The Woolworth would be the world's tallest skyscraper for over fifteen years, until the 927-foot, seventy-two-story Bank of Manhattan was completed just several city streets below, at 40 Wall Street.

Below: Corporate splendor: F. W. Woolworth's office. (*Albert Wilhelmi Collection*)

Right: In 1929, the Woolworth Building had a new neighbor—the forty-two-story Transportation Building was created slightly to the south. (*Albert Wilhelmi Collection*)

Left: The Woolworth Building's imposing lobby. (*Albert Wilhelmi Collection*)

Below: Floodlit to the very top, the Woolworth was one of the first city buildings to use night-time lighting. This view dates from 1916. (*Der Scutt Collection*)

The observation deck on the fifty-seventh floor remained very popular until it was closed in 1941, due to security imposed by the Second World War, and was never reopened. By the 1930s, Manhattan had its fair share of skyscraper observatories that included the Empire State, Chrysler, RCA, Cities Service, and Bank of Manhattan towers. Even the forty-nine-story Chanin Building, located at East 42nd Street and Lexington Avenue, had an upper observation deck as did the forty-two-story Williamsburgh Savings Bank over in Brooklyn.

The Woolworth was, to many, not just beautiful, but exceptionally beautiful. It had a distinct resemblance to the great cathedrals of Europe and it was soon dubbed 'The Cathedral of Commerce.' The stately Woolworth rose majestically and was cast in limestone-colored, glazed architectural terra-cotta panels. Strongly articulated piers that were carried right to pyramidal top gave the building an elegant, upward thrust. At the top, the Gothic detailing was specially oversized and could be seen from the street below. The building underwent an extensive four-year restoration in 1977–81. Much of the original, badly worn and weathered terra-cotta was replaced with concrete. Much of the Gothic ornamentation was also removed.

Within, the building was just as stylized. The main lobby—dubbed 'one of the most spectacular of the early 20th century in New York City' and once a tourist attraction on its own—hinted not only of success and wealth, but also grandeur. It is covered in Skyros-veined marble with a vaulted ceiling, mosaics, a stained glass ceiling light, and bronze fittings. Over the lobby balconies are murals 'Labor & Commerce.' One shows Cass Gilbert holding a model of the building while another depicts Woolworth himself counting nickels. Woolworth's richly decorated private office has been preserved to this day.

The Woolworth Company, by then itself much-diminished in size, sold the building in 1998 after eighty-five years. A small presence remained for a few years afterward through a Foot Locker shop, an offshoot of the Woolworth Company. The Witkoff Group, a real estate firm, bought the building for $155 million. During the destruction of the nearby World Trade Center on 11 September 2001, the Woolworth suffered broken windows and had some damage to the top turret.

THE WOOLWORTH BUILDING AND CITY HALL PARK
BY NIGHT, NEW YORK CITY.

Right: A night-time view of the Woolworth Building,
City Hall, and the Singer Building dated 1915.
(*Albert Wilhelmi Collection*)

Below: The stylized, highly detailed main entrance of the
Woolworth Building along Broadway.
(*Albert Wilhelmi Collection*)

OPPOSITE PAGE:

A stunning example of early skyscraper architecture—the
Woolworth as seen in 1912. (*Albert Wilhelmi Collection*)

With changing times and demands for aging skyscrapers, the top thirty floors of the Woolworth were sold for $68 million in 2012. The new owners, Alchemy Properties, planned to develop those upper floors into luxury apartments and to create a five-floor penthouse at the top. The project was branded Woolworth Tower Residences. In 2014, the $110 million price tag for the penthouse made it the highest amount ever for an apartment in Lower Manhattan.

In 2015, the elegant Woolworth Building was less visible on the city's downtown skyline. Two very tall apartment towers obscure much of it and it is, of course, greatly dwarfed by the nearby World Trade Center, which is more than twice the height of the beloved Woolworth Building.

Above: Part of an admission ticket to the observatory atop the sixty-story Woolworth Building. (*Albert Wilhelmi Collection*)

Left: The splendid Gothic tower. (*Albert Wilhelmi Collection*)

Seven

GERMAN BEHEMOTHS
Imperator, Vaterland, and Bismarck

IN 1990, I WAS FORTUNATE to have stayed at the Royal Automobile Club in London. That classic structure, that grand institution, evoked the glories of bygone London. It was classic architecture, stately style, and, amidst its splendors and comforts, it included a lavish indoor swimming pool. A grand, extravagant creation in marble with Greek columns was the creation of brilliant designer Charles Mewes. That same pool, in a similar style, reappeared soon afterward in the great German liners *Imperator*, *Vaterland*, and *Bismarck*.

Years later, in the summer of 1999 during a stop at Liverpool, I had a special outing, going north to Lancaster, then to north-west England, to a local pub that had historic interest; the pub contained some of the wood paneling from the Cunard liner *Berengaria*, which in her prior life had been the innovative German flagship *Imperator*. The panels had been extracted from the ship before she was scrapped in 1938, and then sold at auction. They are, in a small way, a link to one of the greatest of the floating palaces.

By 1910, the Germans wanted to surpass the British more than ever, specifically regarding those big Cunard and White Star liners, and not only for corporate competition, but for national prestige. The Hamburg-America Line in particular, under the guidance of shipping genius Albert Ballin, was determined to build bigger and bigger liners. The company planned three successively larger liners and all with the gleaming eye of approval of the Kaiser himself. They selected a three-ship design. The forward funnel, aboard the 52,100 gross ton

Imperator, alone measured 69 feet above the upper deck, and ranked as one of the tallest funnels fitted to a passenger ship. Later, these three funnels would create balance problems and had to be cut down by as much as 9 feet. Two masts towered at each end of the ship. Along her decks were eighty-three lifeboats and two motor launches (figures prompted by the *Titanic* tragedy), four four-bladed propellers that could make 185 revolutions per minute, and twin engine rooms that were 69 and 95 feet long and had bunkers for 8,500 tons of coal.

The Kaiser launched the new liner at Hamburg in May 1912 and she set off in the following spring on her maiden crossing to America. The public was dazzled by her and her statistics such as having quarters for as many as 4,594 total passengers—908 in first class, 972 second class, 942 third class, and 1,772 steerage. After all, first-class traffic on the Atlantic was rising and westbound immigration to the USA was equally promising (nearly 1 million crossed to New York in 1914 alone). Clearly, two even larger sisters were needed.

Some 40,000 people attended the launching of the second, larger German giant, the 54,300-ton *Vaterland*. She was built at the renowned Blohm & Voss shipyard at Hamburg and was launched in April 1913. Again, the public was fascinated by her statistics and details. There were 1.5 million rivets used in her construction, the ship's bunkers held up to 9,000 tons of coal, and there was space for 12,000 tons of cargo. The 1,180-member crew was headed by a commodore, two assistant captains, seven nautical officers, and

Above: Fitting out and nearly complete in 1913, Germany's *Imperator* would rank as the largest ship of any kind then afloat—52,117 tons and 919 feet in length. (*Hapag-Lloyd*)

Left: The second German giant, the *Vaterland,* later sailed as the *Leviathan* for the United States Lines. A prize of war, she was the largest vessel under the American flag. (*Author's Collection*)

OPPOSITE PAGE:

Tiny but powerful tugs carefully swing the *Berengaria* into her berth at Pier 54, New York. In this view from 1929, the brand new Chrysler Building can be seen at the top left. (*Port Authority of New York and New Jersey*)

Below: The earliest superliners were actually German—ships such as the 655-foot-long *Kaiser Wilhelm der Grosse* of 1897. Artist Don Stoltenberg created this painting to commemorate the grand age of 'German greyhounds' on the Atlantic. (*Donald Stoltenberg Collection*)

Above: An otherwise useless ornament, the mounted eagle and globe pushed the *Imperator*'s overall length by 20 feet so as to ensure it would surpass her nearest rival, the 901 feet of Britain's *Aquitania*. (*Hapag-Lloyd*)

Left: A postcard of another big German, the 707-foot-long *Kaiser Wilhelm II*, completed in 1903. She could carry 1,888 passengers on week-long passages between Germany and New York. (*Author's Collection*)

twenty-nine engineers. For transatlantic luxury, she was the top of her class; the accommodations in first class included a winter garden, social hall, large dining saloon, grill room, and smoking room. There was an entire row of shops, a bank, a travel bureau, and an indoor pool gymnasium complex. There were 752 beds in the first-class staterooms, headed by a pair of two extremely luxurious

Seen outbound along the Hudson River with the Woolworth and Singer buildings all but dead ahead, the mighty *Imperator* had eighty-three lifeboats for a total of 4,594 passengers (in four classes) and 1,000 crew. (*Hapag-Lloyd*)

imperial suites and ten deluxe apartments. In all, the 950-foot-long *Vaterland* could carry up to 4,909 passengers.

Sadly, however, the Germans were not able to enjoy their third giant liner, 'the Big Three' as they became known. Launched in June 1914 as the *Bismarck*, she was the largest of the three at 56,500 tons and 956 feet in length. But weeks later the First World War started and so the ship sat at her builder's yard, a rusting shell of what was intended to be the world's largest and one of the most luxurious ships. At the war's end in 1918–19, the three German giants were in the Allied hands as reparations—the *Imperator* to Cunard, to become the *Berengaria*; the *Vaterland* to the United States and soon sailing as the *Leviathan*; and the *Bismarck* completed as the *Majestic* for White Star.

The three ships finished sailing just before the start of the Second World War. The *Berengaria* sailed on until being sold to scrappers in 1938 and with her final remains being finished-off in 1946. The *Leviathan* went to the wreckers in 1938, while the *Majestic*—used as a moored cadet-training ship from 1936—caught fire and sank in 1939, with the burnt-out wreckage broken up between 1940 and 1943.

Right: A hotel that floats—first-class grandeur aboard the *Majestic*. (*Norman Knebel Collection*)

Below right: Something of a shipboard novelty: the imposing indoor Pompeian pool aboard the *Majestic*—salt water, a spectators' gallery, and a lighted glass ceiling that imitated daylight. (*Norman Knebel Collection*)

Opposite page:

Above left: Getting away from Pier 59, New York, the towering *Majestic* is seen on a cold, wintery afternoon. (*Cunard*)

Above right: In a photo dated 1932, a passenger arriving on the Italian liner *Rex* photographed New York's Chelsea Piers. Two giant liners, the 882-foot-long *Olympic* (left) and 956-foot-long *Leviathan*, are berthed at Pier 59. To the left, the newly completed 1,250-foot-high Empire State Building dominates the city skyline. (*Maurizio Eliseo Collection*)

Below: Intended to be the third German giant, the *Bismarck*, the ship never entered service until ceded to the British as reparations and then completed in 1922 as White Star line's *Majestic*. At 56,551 tons and 950 feet in length, she was advertised as 'the biggest liner afloat,' a distinction that indeed brought her additional passengers. In this 1925 view, the liner is seen passing the Lower Manhattan skyline. (*Cronican Arroyo Collection*)

Eight

AUTOMOTIVE STYLE
The Chrysler Building

ON A SUN-FILLED AUTUMN AFTERNOON in 1982, I joined fellow members of New York City's Art Deco Society for a unique occasion—a visit to the space that had been the Cloud Club high above the midtown city on the sixty-sixth floor. We were in the upper turret of the famed Chrysler, and although the space had long since been stripped, almost to the bone (making it look bare and uninviting), it was still one of New York City's most beautiful and beloved buildings. We even had an added treat—opening the windows in those upper eyelid-like openings, carefully peering out, and looking over the midtown skyline. These days, in an age of high security, visitors can barely enter the Chrysler Building's lobby.

With a recent surge in construction of tall buildings, the Chrysler is perhaps less readily visible. However, it remains an especially beautiful, striking, and evocative structure. 'People just love the Chrysler Building,' said the late, Jersey City-based architect Ted Conrad. 'They look at it and just about smile. It is beauty, it is style, it is the American dream!' Albert Wilhelmi noted:

Architects Severance and Van Allen had been partners, but then split and thereafter tried to outdo each other. Almost each day, they would change the heights of their respective towers, 40 Wall Street and the Chrysler Building. They wanted to keep one another guessing. Yasuo Matsui was the real designer of 40 Wall Street and he got the final credit, however. The Chrysler won out, of course, with its secret spire. The Chrysler was also much more innovative. It was actually futuristic. Even to this day, it is slightly over the top. It was, however, not fully appreciated at first when it was new. There is an added irony: Van Allen gave Chrysler the world's tallest building, but then Van Allen had to sue Chrysler to get paid for his work.

Albert Wilhelmi added:

The Chrysler Building was both very innovative and very distinctive. It is perhaps best compared to the *Ile de France*, which, in 1927, introduced Art Deco decor to the high seas and subsequently to almost all liners, and then including its bold exterior as well, it is best compared to the spectacular French liner *Normandie*.

The Chrysler Building is one of the greatest expressions of Art Deco. It often ranks in the lists of greatest as well as favorite buildings. It was purposely designed as the headquarters of the Chrysler Corporation and used by them from its opening in May 1930 to the mid-1950s. The building was not owned or paid for by the corporation, but by Walter P. Chrysler himself so that his family could inherit it.

The seventy-seven-floor building began construction on 19 September 1928, and rose quickly, usually at the rate of four floors per week. Originally designed to be 807 feet in height, plans changed several times—including 925 feet and finally to 1,046 feet.

Above left: Voted in recent years as the favorite older skyscraper by a committee of architects, the Chrysler Building rose in the late 1920s as a symbol of moderne, contemporary elegance, and the future. (*Author's Collection*)

Above right: In this October 1946 photo, the 1941 flagship *Queen Elizabeth* has just arrived to resume post-war commercial service. The 1,046 foot tall Chrysler Building stands above. The building to the right is fifty-three-floor 500 Lexington Avenue on the far taller Empire State Building (*Cunard*)

Far left: Above the entrance to the Chrysler Building. (*Author's Collection*)

Near left: The iconic eyelid windows at the top of the Chrysler Building. (*Albert Wilhelmi Collection*)

In less than two years of construction, almost 400,000 rivets were used and over 3.8 million bricks. Intended originally to have a glass crown at the top, exterior detailing changed as well and was finally completed with symbols of the machine age of the 1920s, but also with an automotive theme. Highlight features include gargoyles modeled after Chrysler products such as the hood ornaments of Plymouth automobiles. The corners of the sixty-first floor are graced with eagles and 1929 Chrysler radiator caps on the thirty-first floor. Constructed of masonry and metal cladding, the building has 3,862 windows. Most distinctive is the tower itself, constructed into seven concentric members with transitional setbacks one behind the other. The stainless cladding is ribbed and riveted into a radiating sunburst pattern of triangular windows. The entire crown, often seen gleaming and shining, is clad in a silvery 'Enduro KA-2' metal, an austenitic stainless steel developed by Krupp in Germany. The steel was marketed under the trade name 'Nirosta.'

Architect van Allen especially wanted to make this building the world's tallest and he was deeply troubled by 40 Wall Street being the same height as well as being designed by his rival and former partner, H. M. Craig Severance. In response and in great secrecy, Van Alen obtained official permission to add a 125-foot-tall spire to the tower. To maintain the secrecy of the plan, he would have the spire constructed inside the upper frame of the building itself. The spire was delivered to the site in four sections and on 29 October 1929,

Near right: Like a spaceship, the seventy-seven-floor Chrysler Building soars above the midtown Manhattan skyline, it also looks like it is making a take-off. (*ALF Collection*)

Far right: Grand style: the extraordinary Chrysler Building and its significant spire. (*Albert Wilhelmi Collection*)

the bottom section was hoisted upward to the building's dome and lowered onto the sixty-sixth floor. In highly organized efficiency, the remaining sections of the spire were hoisted and then promptly riveted to the first one in sequential order and all in just ninety minutes. When opened on 20 May 1930, the Chrysler was the tallest building in the world and the first to exceed 1,000 feet in height. However, within just less than a year, on 1 May 1931, the 1,250-foot tall Empire State Building opened. The Chrysler Building moved to second place.

The public observatory on the seventy-first floor was closed in 1945 and the three-floor Cloud Club, a private restaurant on the sixty-sixth to sixty-eighth floors, closed its doors in the 1970s. The very top floors, from seventy-two through seventy-seven, are mostly stairwells to the spire, mechanical spaces, and had been used for radio as well as television broadcasting. WCBS Television broadcast from the top of the Chrysler Building until the early 1950s and radio stations such as WPAT until the early 1970s. There is no longer commercial broadcasting from the Chrysler.

The building was sold in 1953 by the Chrysler family to a succession of varied owners that included Massachusetts Life Insurance Company, the Travelers Insurance Group, real estate consortiums, Cooper Union, and, by 2008, 90 percent of the building was used by the Abu Dhabi Investment Council. The building was extensively renovated inside and out during 1978–79, and the spire was restored in 1995.

Far left: High above East 42nd Street, famed photographer Margaret Bourke-White appears from one of the automotive gargoyles. (*Author's Collection*)

Above middle: A TWA plane flies over Manhattan in 1938. The Chrysler Building is to the right. (*Port Authority of New York and New Jersey*)

Left: New additions to the East Side of Midtown by the early 1930s—from left to right: the Lincoln Building, Chanin Building, the Chrysler Building, and the Daily News Building. (*Der Scutt Collection*)

Below middle: Looking east in 1965, the Empire State Building is on the far left and the Chrysler Building in the center. (*ALF Collection*)

Below: Enchanting Manhattan at dusk on a winter's night in 1958. The seventy-story RCA Building is in the center, the Chrysler on the left, and the Empire State Building on the far right. (*Author's Collection*)

Nine

BIG LINERS BETWEEN THE WARS

THE FRENCH LINE'S *ILE DE France* was the first large liner to be built after the First World War. She was launched in 1926, eight years after the war ended. The *Ile*—as she was so often called—was not only the first new Atlantic luxury liner, but also the first of a generation of new 'super ships'. However, this 43,153-ton vessel was not intended to be the largest or longest or fastest. Even her exterior was quite ordinary, featuring three funnels and two tall masts. The great excitement concerning the 1,786-passenger *Ile de France* was her interior decor. There had never been a liner quite like her.

Shipboard decoration had previously been based on shore-side styles—castles, town houses, and English country homes. There were even some dabbling in the exotic Arabian, Egyptian, and even Moorish concoctions. The basic intent was to remind passengers of shore, to help them cope with a rolling or pitching ship in a violent ocean storm.

The 791-foot-long *Ile de France*, which first arrived in New York in June 1927, represented a new age. She was an individual, a revolutionary, the trendsetter of her time. She inaugurated so-called 'ocean liner style'—moderne, early Art Deco, on the high seas. Her style was not based on shore-side design and decor, but a floating, luxurious resort in itself. Soon, by the 1930s, shore-side structures were often copying the great liners and especially the *Ile de France*.

Largely underwritten by the French government (but operated by the Compagnie Generale Transatlantique, CGT or the French Line),

the *Ile de France* was intended to showcase the best in French art and design. Built at St Nazaire, great excitement prevailed even before her commissioning. Preliminary literature hinted of her innovative grandeur and style. Even before setting-off on her first crossing to America, reviews were highly enthusiastic and very positive.

The 390 first-class suites and cabins were decorated in many different styles. Her public rooms were eclectic as well as spacious; copying the styles first seen at the International Exposition of Modern Industrial & Decorative Arts held in Paris in 1925, the *Ile de France* smoothly introduced a new age in liner decoration, an era of angular and steel-tubed furniture, sweeping columns, blonde woods and lacquered panels, glossy floors, indirect lighting, and such special distinctions as the longest bar on all the seas. In the three-deck-high, first-class restaurant, where there were no carved eagles or gilded cherubs, was likened to a modern-day version of an ancient Greek temple. There was a sweeping grand staircase as a dramatic entrance and all the chairs were purposely made slightly smaller so as to make the entire room appear larger. There were eight courses for dinner and the Beluga was served in silver bowls. The main foyer was even higher—four decks in total—and an imitated Gothic chapel had fourteen pillars and Stations of the Cross. Every amenity was included—even a merry-go-round for younger passengers.

Berthing aboard the *Ile de France* was arranged in three classes: first, cabin, and an upgraded third class. Steerage had virtually disappeared

by the mid-'20s following great limitations on foreign immigration enacted in the new American Quota System. Liner companies were forced to rethink their austere, less-expensive lower-deck quarters and create more colorful and comfortable third-class accommodation. In the late 1920s, it was $70 per person in a third-class cabin aboard the *Ile de France* for a weeklong crossing of the Atlantic. Third class soon appealed to budget-minded tourists, especially Americans heading off for a summer in Europe. The first class section was expectedly sumptuous and aboard the *Ile de France,* included the greatest array of penthouses and suites. By 1935, the ship had carried more first-class passengers than any other trans-Atlantic liner. The *Ile de France* was described by legions of travelers as 'the cheeriest way to cross the Atlantic.' The food was exceptional, and it was said that more sea gulls followed the *Ile de France* than any other ship.

The *Ile de France* was the beginning, the innovator and raised the bar in all ways for great ocean liners. Used as a troopship during the Second World War, she was restored to her glorious, well-served, and superbly fed self in 1948–49 and sailed for thirty-two years until she was retired and then demolished in Japan in 1959.

Most observers would not have guessed that, by 1929, the Germans would have rejoined what were called 'the ocean liner sweepstakes.' After losing the war in 1918 and then stripped of just about all their tonnage, the Germans were left with one liner that could play the

Above: Outbound from lower Manhattan: a well-wisher is unusually posed high atop Battery Park as the *Ile de France* passes by. (*Author's Collection*)

Left: Ocean-going comfort: a first-class stateroom aboard the decoratively innovative *Ile de France*. (*French Line*)

role of national flagship, the 32,500-ton *Columbus*, commissioned in 1924. An otherwise fine and solid ship, she was not, however, distinctive in any way. There were plans for two sister ships. There was still a need for big liner companies to have the fast ships to run a weekly 'express service' to and from New York — one calling in

After the Second World War, the German *Europa* was resurrected and refitted as the French *Liberte*. It is the 936-foot-long ship's return to Atlantic service. The date is August 1950 and the Woolworth Building can be seen at the top right. (*Moran Towing and Transportation Co.*)

each direction and one in motion at sea. However, by 1925, those early drawings for two further liners were revised. Ambitions were certainly heightened, and the mood was more dramatic and more competitive; the revived Germans wanted renewed maritime distinction. The two new liners would instead be 50,000 tons and, while not the largest afloat, they would have the most powerful maritime machinery to date. They would be the 'German monsters,' the fastest liners in the world and take the prized Blue Riband for speed from Britain and from Cunard's *Mauretania*. It was altogether very much like the Singer Building being succeeded by the Metropolitan Life Building, then by the Woolworth Building, the Chrysler Building and finally, in the early '30s, by the Empire State Building.

The very best German designers and engineers competed for the honor of creating these new national symbols, which were launched a day apart in the summer of 1928 as the *Bremen* and *Europa*. Their hulls would be long and sleek, and introduced the bulbous bow, a novel design feature that reduced drag at sea and added to a ship's speed. At times, the ships looked almost sinister, especially with their twin squat stacks. They were soon called 'greyhounds'—almost urgently crossing the seas with their German might and appearance.

Publicists at the North German Lloyd, the ship's owners, prodded by a much-interested government in Berlin, had a dramatic early plan—the two liners crossing on their maiden voyages together and having both take the Riband from the *Mauretania*. They provided a powerful symbol of Germany's post-war recovery, skill, and highly technological abilities. However, the plan never came to fruition. While being outfitted at Hamburg, in March 1929, the 936-foot-long *Europa* was badly damaged by fire and might even have had to be scrapped. At the very least, she was much-delayed. So, the *Bremen* crossed alone (in July 1929), but stealing the trophy from the *Mauretania* with a record-breaking time of four days and seventeen hours. It was two hours less than the *Mauretania*'s record established twenty-two years before. Ministers in Berlin were beaming. A congratulatory message was sent from the older Cunarder to the new German.

The 51,656-ton *Bremen* made the initial headlines, was slightly better known, and seen as the most successful of the pair. The *Europa* took the record in March 1930, but then the title passed back to the slightly faster *Bremen* before going to the Italian *Rex* in the summer of 1933. Unfortunately, the two liners would see less than a decade of service under the German flag. Laid-up when the Second World War began in Europe in late 1939, the *Bremen* was destroyed by fire in March 1941 and her remains later scrapped; the *Europa*, not used by the Nazi high command during the war years, was captured by the American invasion forces in May 1945, used briefly as the trooper USS *Europa*, but then later ceded to the French as reparations. Refitted and de-Germanized, she sailed as the French flagship *Liberte* until 1961, when, in creaking old age, she was scrapped in Italy.

Mussolini's Italy joined the ocean liner sweepstakes in the summer of 1932. The Genoa-based Italian Line introduced the *Rex* and later her fleetmate, the *Conte di Savoia*, but they were quite different from each other. The *Rex* was both larger and faster; the latter was thought by some to be better looking on the outside and having slightly better appointments within. Originally ordered by separate Italian ship owners, they became running mates from completion onward after the Mussolini government merged their owners—to reduce costs and lessen competition. The Italian liners were to herald, again with Mussolini's blessings, a new era in Mediterranean passenger service. The Mediterranean route had always been bypassed by travelers who tended to use the Northern passage. The Italians soon mounted a large, very colorful advertising campaign highlighting the glories of what was called the 'sunny southern route to Europe.' The Italian Riviera, with its quaint little harbors and special beaches, was an obvious link as well as lure. Onboard these new Italian super liners, the first to have several outdoor pools, sand was even scattered around the decks to convey the message. A name, the Lido, was borrowed from Venice and soon the top deck was the Lido Deck. The marketing message was perfect: 'The Riviera comes to meet you on board the *Rex* and *Conte di Savoia*.' There were rows of reclining deck chairs and colored umbrellas, and with small armies

Top left: The German superliners *Bremen* and *Europa*, introduced in 1929–30, hinted of the new moderne in ocean liner design. Their long, low superstructures were capped by two squat funnels (which soon had to be heightened because of problems on upper, open decks with smoke and soot). (*Author's Collection*)

Above left: German decor: the Main Lounge aboard the 51,656-grt *Bremen*, first commissioned in the summer of 1929. She could carry 2,200 passengers, divided into three classes. (*Hapag-Lloyd*)

Right: The same ship, seen from Hoboken and with the Empire State Building behind, the *Liberte* heads to sea in this view dated February 1958. (*Port Authority of New York and New Jersey*)

of stripe-shirted deck stewards to cater to the passengers' needs. Indeed, the *Rex* and *Conte di Savoia* were not just big 'floating hotels,' but 'floating resorts' as well.

Teething problems have beset many liners, sometimes on the maiden voyage or in a ship's maiden year. In September 1932, the 880-foot-long *Rex* (approximately 150 feet shorter than the Chrysler Building) was still in the confines of the Mediterranean, during her west-bound maiden voyage to New York, when her engines failed. The 51,062-tonner was just approaching Gibraltar when she was crippled and the Italians grew worried as well as mortified. The 2,358-passenger ship had to wait three days for repairs, and all while many of her passengers grew impatient, lost their enthusiasm, and even fled to other ships. Jimmy Walker, the mayor of New York, took a train to Cherbourg and boarded the German *Europa* for a more reliable journey home.

Secretly, the Italians had been hoping to capture the Blue Riband on the *Rex*'s maiden trip, but now that had to wait; repairs became the priority. Once at New York, there were more problems—the new flagship had no power. While celebratory dinners, parties, and tours were underway, the big liner received emergency power from a railway barge moored alongside. Meanwhile, other, if smaller, Italian liners were speeding to New York to deliver spare parts to the troubled *Rex*.

It took almost a full year, but in August 1933 the *Rex* finally captured the Blue Riband. She took it from the German *Bremen* with a speed of almost 29 knots. Her record run was four days and thirteen hours.

The 48,502-ton *Conte di Savoia* made her maiden crossing two months after the *Rex*, in November 1932. All seemed to go well until, when 900 miles west of the American mainland, an outlet valve below the waterline jammed and then blew a very worrisome hole in the side of 814-foot-long liner (slightly more than the height of the Woolworth Building). In a matter of minutes, seawater rushed in through the hole and began to flood the liner's dynamo compartment. Kept secret from the happy passengers above, it was soon realized that the ship could sink in as little as five hours. Fortunately, the crew was resourceful. One member, showing exceptional bravery, went below and filled the hole with cement. The ship was able to continue safely to New York, the passengers were informed and that courageous crew member given a good-sized booty.

Great and grand Italians, the *Rex* (left), *Conte di Savoia*, and *Conte Grande* berthed together at Genoa in 1933. (Richard Faber Collection)

Outbound in September 1935 from New York's Pier 60, well-wishers see off the mighty Italian liner *Conte di Savoia*. (*ALF Collection*)

It is well-known that the Atlantic Ocean can be among the roughest of passages. While ship owners dislike delays and fear damages to their ship, the passengers themselves dislike a rolling or pitching ship, crashing tableware and missed meals, and, of course, the discomfort of the dreaded *mal de mer*. When looking for some distinction for its second new liner, an innovative gyro-stabilizer system was fitted aboard the *Conte di Savoia*. Unlike any other big liner, the Italians could advertise the 2,200-passenger liner as the 'roll-less ship'. It was actually a repeat of the earlier *Olympic* and *Titanic*. White Star Line wanted an added distinction for its second new liner and so the *Titanic* was called 'unsinkable'. The *Savoia*'s new gyro-stabilizer system was in fact the first on a big liner and so she was advertised as offering 'the smoothest sail on the Atlantic'. But, at best, the system was very limited, less successful than the Italians had planned. It could not be used on the westbound trips to New York, for example, because of prevailing winds. Consequently, passengers aboard the 27-knot *Conte di Savoia* were often unpleasantly surprised to find the liner tossing and pitching like any other ship.

Withdrawn from service by June 1940 because of the war in Europe, these Italians were both later bombed, set afire, sunk, and ruined beyond repair. The last remains of the salvaged *Conte di Savoia* were cut-up in 1950 and for the *Rex* by 1958.

Below: The 1930s was an era of especially high style. Here is the famed poster, dated 1931, of the French liner *L'Atlantique*. Considered a great example of Art Deco design and art, it was created by French artist Cassandre. (*Author's Collection*)

Left: Cities at sea—the chapel aboard the 2,200-passenger *Conte di Savoia*. (*Richard Faber Collection*)

Ten

HIGH ABOVE WALL STREET
The Bank of Manhattan and Cities Services Buildings

IN THE FRIGID AIR OF a January morning in 2012, we had a prized invitation—to visit the top floors of the otherwise all but empty former AIG Building in Lower Manhattan. I was thrilled and most grateful. It is one of my all-time favorite buildings, and a very distinctive one at that. In its previous life, as the Cities Service Building, it was the third tallest building in all of New York City and the tallest in Lower Manhattan. It is also one of the grandest of Art Deco creations. On that winter visit, we toured the upper floors, the stripped down offices, the disorderly executive dining rooms, and, at the very top, on the sixty-sixth floor, the former observatory. Even in its emptiness and desolation (AIG had gone bankrupt and was forced to vacate the tower), it was all great style, fascinating design, power, and the highest example of 'skyscraper style.' As we stepped out onto the open-air decks, we could all but touch some of the other nearby towers, including its cousin of sorts, the former Bank of Manhattan Building, another favorite of mine. I could not leave out these buildings in this study.

For less than two months, in April–May 1930, the Bank of Manhattan Building was the world's tallest skyscraper. It surpassed the Woolworth Tower, previously the tallest, by well over 100 feet and more than ten floors. Standing at 40 Wall Street and located between Nassau and William streets, construction on the building started in the twilight of the high-spirited '20s. Original plans were for a building of 840 feet (or a mere 48 feet taller than the nearby Woolworth Building, then still the world's tallest) and sixty-eight

floors, and altogether two feet taller than the projected Chrysler Building farther north, in midtown Manhattan along East 42nd Street. The architects of the Bank of Manhattan tower were worried, however. The Chrysler was a serious threat. They wanted to be sure their building would be 'world's tallest'. Plans for the Bank of Manhattan were changed, creating a slightly taller skyscraper of 927 feet and seventy-one floors. Victory would be too short-lived, however. Within a month, the Bank of Manhattan tower was listed as the world's second tallest skyscraper.

'The Bank of Manhattan was also a very conservative building, one almost harking back to the nearby Woolworth Building,' added Albert Wilhelmi.

Capped by a pyramid top with a lantern and needle-like spire atop it, the Bank of Manhattan was surpassed by the Chrysler using, what some called, 'a secret weapon.' With both buildings under construction at the same time, a 125-foot-tall stainless spire was secretly assembled in the Chrysler's tower section and then hoisted into place. The seventy-seven-story Chrysler now stood 1,046 feet above Lexington Avenue, and 119 feet taller than the Bank of Manhattan. On opening day, 28 May 1930, the Chrysler was proclaimed the world's tallest building. However, there had been a debate over the distinction; the architects of 40 Wall Street claimed that the building's observatory was 100 feet above the uppermost floor of the Chrysler. The latter's spire was inaccessible and merely decorative.

Above left: One of the most striking of the new age of Manhattan skyscrapers was the Cities Services Building, located at 70 Pine Street in Lower Manhattan. Seen from across the East River, from the Brooklyn waterfront, it rose to 950 feet, making it the third tallest building in the world when completed in 1932. (*Port Authority of New York and New Jersey*)

Above right: With sixty-six floors, the new tower could be seen for miles around. (*Author's Collection*)

Left. The kingdom emerges. The lower Manhattan skyline as seen from an inbound ocean liner. (*Author's Collection*)

Far left: High above: a splendid aerial photo of lower Manhattan dated 1939. (*Port Authority of New York and New Jersey*)

Near left: The lower Manhattan skyline, the cluster of towers was a great marking and focal point for arriving ships. In this view, dated 1933, the liner *Washington* is arriving on its maiden voyage. (*Richard Faber Collection*)

Far left, above: Stephen Card's superb painting of the liner *America* passing lower Manhattan. (*Stephen Card Collection*)

Far left, below: A Zeppelin passes over lower Manhattan in 1936. (*Port Authority of New York and New Jersey*)

Middle: A lantern and spire are affixed to the very top of the seventy-two-floor Bank of Manhattan Building. (*Albert Wilhelmi Collection*)

Above right: Dramatic skies over the Hudson: a bleak morning in 1939 of the river, shipping, and the biggest trio of towers in lower Manhattan—the Woolworth, Cities Services, and Bank of Manhattan. (*Author's Collection*)

Left: Dusk in 1958. (*Author's Collection*)

The debate lingered, but soon no longer mattered—the 1,250-foot-tall, 102-floor Empire State Building was completed eleven months later. Quickly, the Chrysler slipped to second place and the Bank of Manhattan to third (and then, rather quickly, to fourth when the nearby, 950-foot Cities Service Building opened in 1932).

In an accident far less remembered than an aircraft's crash into the Empire State Building in July 1945, a US Army airplane rammed the north side of the Bank of Manhattan building on the foggy night of 20 May 1946. It struck the fifty-eighth floor on the north side and left a 10 × 20-foot hole in masonry. All five aboard the plane were killed. While parts of the aircraft, as well as pieces of masonry, fell into the street below, none of the 2,000 people in the tower were injured. Like the crash into the Empire State Building, fog and poor visibility were blamed as the causes.

After the Bank of Manhattan merged with Chase Manhattan Bank in 1970s, the building was relisted as 40 Wall Street. It was sold in 1982, to buyers who, it was later discovered, were acting on behalf of Ferdinand and Imelda Marcos, the president and first lady of the Philippines. Later, when Marcos was removed from power and his American assets frozen, 40 Wall Street fell into limbo, neglect, even deep decay. In 1995, it was bought by real estate mogul Donald Trump, who renamed it The Trump Building and planned to make thirty or so floors into apartments and leave the remaining four as commercial space, but the residential conversion never occurred.

Like glittering jewels, lower Manhattan sparkled. (*Author's Collection*)

Eight years later, in 2003, Trump offered the building for sale. The asking price was over $300 million. Unsold, Trump suggested four years later that the building was worth over $600 million.

The Trump Building has been fully restored in recent years and this has included an exterior cleaning and renewal. Although there are several taller buildings now nearby, 40 Wall Street stands out, especially in sunlight. It has a radiance, a presence, and a certain individuality. A single red light in the lantern at the very top was relighted, after almost thirty years, in January 2015.

A little more than two years after the Bank of Manhattan tower was completed, it had a sort of sister tower—the Cities Service Building— which rose quite close by at 70 Pine Street. It was created especially for that oil company, by the oil and gas baron, Henry Latham Doherty. It was designed by Clinton & Russell in high Art Deco style.

Right: The very top of the Cities Services Building has been called futuristic, Jazz Deco, even Captain Video in style. It is topped by a stainless mast. (*Albert Wilhelmi Collection*)

Below: A cold winter's morning in 2011: the author atop the former Cities Service Building. (*Albert Wilhelmi Collection*)

The four new skyscrapers in Lower Manhattan of the early 1930s: City Bank Farmers Trust Company (left), Cities Service, Bank of Manhattan and, shortest of the four, Irving Trust. (*Port Authority of New York and New Jersey*)

Rising sixty-seven floors and 952 feet, the Cities Service Building was a highpoint in Manhattan's skyscraper community and, as the Great Depression took a deeper hold and world events changed, it was the last tower built in Lower Manhattan prior to the outbreak of the Second World War. It was the third tallest skyscraper in the world, surpassed only by the Empire State Building and the Chrysler Building, until the completion in the early 1970s of the World Trade Center. Following the attack and collapse of the Trade Center towers on 11 September 2001, the building once again became the tallest in Lower Manhattan.

A sleek, slender tower—clad in limestone—is capped by a tiered collection of outdoor platforms. At the very top is a glass-enclosed observatory topped-off by a stainless mast. The tower was floodlit by night for many years and the mast fitted with a flashing red aviation light. The observatory, a public space in the early years, was used later for corporate entertainment. Within, and including a handsome lobby, the tower was rather famously built with double-decker elevators that serviced two floors at a time. These suited the very slender tower floors with their limited space for multiple shafts. These double-decker elevators were less than successful, however, and were later removed.

This building was not as, say, outrageous as the Chrysler Building, but it too is one of the very best Art Deco designs of all Manhattan

Viewed from the deck of a Hoboken ferry, the towers of lower Manhattan make a grand collection. (*Author's Collection*)

skyscrapers. While under construction, the very top was redesigned and made even more dramatic. It is very Captain Video. It has always been a 'sleeper'. It has never been fully appreciated. It was like the Italian super liner *Conte di Savoia*. It too was largely obscured, even overwhelmed by other big liners, namely the *Rex*, of the same era.

Albert Wilhelmi

Cities Service moved its headquarters to Tulsa in 1976 and sold the tower to AIG, the American International Group. AIG lavishly and almost lovingly looked after the tower, but because of its own serious financial problems by 2008, vacated its offices and sold the building. It was actually sold several times, to various real estate developers, until finally placed in the hands of combination owners: the Luxembourg-based Eastbridge Group and New York-headquartered Rose Associates. Beginning in 2013, 70 Pine Street began a transformation into 644 residential apartments and 132 extended-stay units. Restaurants, retail spaces, a fitness club, and, in the top-floor observatory, a cigar bar were planned. Like several older skyscrapers, the former Cities Service Building lives on in a practical reuse.

Eleven

SUPER SHIPS OF THE 1930s
Normandie, Queen Mary, and Queen Elizabeth

WITHIN FOUR YEARS OF THE maiden voyage of Italy's *Rex* in September 1932, two far larger, faster, more luxurious, and possibly more noteworthy liners had entered Atlantic service. They were the biggest ships yet—record-breakers in almost every way.

With the first plans drawn in the late 1920s, the French produced a super liner to pull out all stops and take all records. The exquisite *Normandie*, the most splendid of all big liners in the '30s, was commissioned in the spring of 1935. Her creators had three goals: to build the first liner to exceed 1,000 feet in length, but also to weigh at least 60,000 tons; to make her the fastest ship on the Atlantic; and, finally, to create a dazzling, stunning floating ambassador of the very best of French design, decoration, and technology. In all these aims, the brilliant, three-funnel *Normandie* succeeded.

While her first steel plates were laid down in January 1931, her construction schedule was delayed by the Great Depression. Due in 1933, she was not commissioned until the spring of 1935. In many ways, she was a great symbol of hope, especially to the French themselves, during those adverse job-and-food short times. Others saw her as 'an expensive extravagance, inexcusable foolishness.' Her name created a string of rumors—*Jean d 'Arc, La Belle France, General Pershing, Napoleon, Pax,* and even *Maurice Chevalier* were said to be considered. However, she was launched in October 1932 as the *Normandie*. She was so massive that the backwash of her 1,028-foot-long unfinished hull (or just 18 feet

shorter than the Chrysler Building) was enough to sweep 100 shipyard workers into the Loire. Already, she was a ship of the dramatic.

When complete, with her stylized, modern profile, the *Normandie*'s tonnage far exceeded the 60,000-ton mark—she was finally placed at over 79,000 tons. As the French predicted, she was the biggest liner in the world. But that triumph was short lived. Word came from across the Channel, from Cunard Line headquarters in Liverpool and from Scottish shipbuilders on the River Clyde, that the first of two new, giant Cunard liners would be at least 80,000 tons. The French were deeply worried—the *Normandie* would be in second place. Consequently, during the French liner's first winter overhaul in 1935–36, she was fitted with a large but unnecessary aft deckhouse. This pushed her tonnage up to 83,400. The new Cunard liner, the *Queen Mary*, was completed in spring 1936 at 80,700 tons. The French had won, at least temporarily. The second big Cunarder, the *Queen Elizabeth*, would be ready in 1940 and bigger still, at 83,600 tons. She would take the record for well over the next fifty years.

The *Normadie* also had her battles of speed. She swept the Atlantic in May 1935 with a record faster than Italy's *Rex*. The French liner average speed stood at 28.92 knots, but just a little more than a year later, the brand new *Queen Mary* did 30.14 knots and so grabbed the prized pennant. In the spring of 1937, the *Normandie* made another attempt and won at 30.9 knots followed by 31.2 knots the following summer. It seemed as if the trophy would remain with the French

Right: The launch of the spectacular *Normandie* at St Nazaire in October 1932. (*French Line*)

Below: Countless artists depicted the great *Normandie*. This is one of French artist Albert Brenet's versions, showing the liner at Le Havre, its homeport. (*Author's Collection*)

until the beloved *Queen Mary* proved faster in 1938 with an average speed of 31.6 knots—the French were beaten.

On the inside, the *Normandie* was acclaimed for her high sense of the moderne, 'the ultimate Art Deco liner' according to at least one writer. Once aboard, the ship was given the highest praises, accolades, and many deep sighs. The main dining room was unlike anything yet seen at sea—a brilliant creation of bronze, hammered glass, and Lalique. It sat 700 diners, rose three decks in height, and in fact was longer than the Hall of Mirrors at Versailles. Needless to say, the menus were beyond compare and offered over 300 choices in eight courses for dinner. The Winter Garden included caged birds, tropical greenery, and sprays of water. The indoor pool measured 80 feet in length and the finest suites included four bedrooms.

Sadly, the *Normandie* saw only four-and-a-half years of service on the Atlantic run, remaining idle at her New York berth for two-and-a-half years only to catch fire on 9 February 1942 while being hastily converted to an Allied troopship. Fireboat water caused her to capsize and then after the war in 1946, her salvaged but reduced remains were cut-up at Port Newark, in New Jersey. In the end, this most beautiful of ships, costing some $60 million, was sold to scrap merchants for a scant $161,000.

Solid, conservative Cunard believed in providing solid, reliable service—not in recreating records for record's sake or in decorative pretensions. They did, however, dream and then plan for the first two-ship express service on the North Atlantic, sailing between Southampton, Cherbourg, and New York. Two, big, very powerful ships were needed.

Above left: Maiden arrival into New York harbor of the 1.028-foot-long *Normandie*, a ship that many appraised as the greatest Atlantic liner of them all. (*South Street Seaport Museum*)

Above right: The *Normandie* could carry up to 1,972 passengers, divided in three classes: first, tourist, and third. First-class guests could enjoy the finest foods in the splendid Lalique and bronze filled main dining room, which was said to be longer than the famed Hall of Mirrors at Versailles. (*French Line*)

Above: During her first visit to New York and berthed at Pier 88, there was a grand open house and thousands toured the luxurious innards of the $60 million *Normandie.* (*French Line*)

Right: Superb quarters: the bedroom of a so-called Apartment de Luxe aboard the *Normandie.* It cost $1,200 per person for a five-night crossing in 1935. (*Richard Faber Collection*)

Left: At 82,799 gross tons, the *Normandie* reigned as the largest and longest liner afloat for a time. (*Author's Collection*)

Above: A gathering of great liners at New York in March 1937: the *Europa* (top), *Rex*, *Normandie*, *Georgic*, and *Berengaria*. (*Author's Collection*)

The first of these, laid down at Clydebank in Scotland in December 1930 was quickly a victim of the Great Depression. The unfinished hull had sat idle for two-and-a-half years before, and with the British government's financial assistance, it could be launched in April 1934 as the *Queen Mary*. She was an immediate symbol—a symbol that went beyond maritime circles. An economically battered Britain, suffering from mass unemployment, food queues, and a dark mood of gloom, saw the new liner as a symbol of hope, even a cause for celebration. She would regain trans-Atlantic for Cunard and the nation, and would be one of the greatest and grandest liners ever to cross the seas.

The 1,018-foot-long ship created a mass of distinction and notation: 10,000,000 rivets, 2,000 portholes, 700 clocks, and as many as fifty-six kinds of genuine woods used in her decoration. Although she used Art Deco decor, she was not as highly luxurious or as extravagant as the *Normandie*. Instead, she was unmistakably a British liner, with

After burning and then capsizing at her Pier 88 berth, the *Normandie* was cut down, righted, and then, in this view from November 1943, towed along the Hudson to await her fate. In fact, the ship's hull was scrapped in 1946–47. Both the Woolworth and Singer buildings stand in the background. (*Author's Collection*)

fireplaces and oversized chairs, lots of flowers, and ritual tea at 4 p.m. The 2,139-bed ship arrived in New York for the first time in May 1936 and quickly settled down to a popular and very profitable life.

Cunard's innovative two-liner express service was to begin in April 1940 with the first arrival of the *Queen Elizabeth,* the second Cunard super ship and the biggest liner afloat at 83,673 tons and 1,031 feet in length. The outbreak of war in Europe changed plans and instead the new liner, joining the likes of the *Queen Mary,* were painted overall in gray and used as 15,000-soldier capacity troopships. The *Elizabeth* and *Mary* would not enter commercial service until 1946–47 and for the next decade were extraordinarily successful ships.

Both *Queens* began to lose money in the early 1960s, the result of unbeatable competition from the airlines. The *Queen Mary* was finally retired in September 1967 and after 1,000 crossings was sold to the City of Long Beach, California, for use as a moored hotel, museum, and collection of shops and restaurants; she remains in this role to date. The *Queen Elizabeth*, which retired in October 1968, did not fare as well. Sold to become a floating hotel and museum at Port Everglades, Florida, the project was never realized and in 1970, the ship was auctioned off to Taiwanese shipping tycoon C. Y. Tung. Renamed *Seawise University*, plans were to use her as a floating university cruise ship. Unfortunately, she never sailed as such, but burned and then capsized in Hong Kong harbor on the eve of her maiden sailing on 9–10 January 1972. Her remains were later scrapped on the spot.

EXPLORE the WORLD'S BIG-
GEST ocean liner afloat SEE the
WORLD'S BIGGEST aircraft ever
built ENTER the WORLD'S BIGGEST self
sustaining aluminum dome AND MORE
three restaurants • six lounges • seventeen
snack bars • thirty five boutiques and shops •
numerous, continuous, informative, exciting
shows and entertainment. It all adds up to a
BIG day of fun and wonder

Far left, above: Art Deco on the high seas: the interiors of the 2,139-passenger *Queen Mary* were described as 'like being in the finest London hotel except that they moved!' This is the first-class main lounge. (*Cunard*)

Far left, below: The *Queen Mary* lives on in gentle and secure retirement in southern California as a hotel, museum, and tourist attraction. (*Hotel Queen Mary*)

Middle: September 1939 and war in Europe has erupted. Many liners remained in the safety of neutral America in New York harbor. Looking from the railway yards of Weehawken, New Jersey, the *Roma* (left), *Queen Mary, Normandie, Ile de France,* and *Champlain* are all but waiting at their West Side piers. (*Author's Collection*)

Above: A section of the smoking room in first class aboard the 81,235-ton Cunard flagship. (*Cunard*)

Left: Seen against a background of the Manhattan skyline, this depiction of the *Queen Mary* is one of size, might, and speed. (*Author's Collection*)

Below left: Great comparison: the 1,018-foot-long *Queen Mary* as if fitted into London's Trafalgar Square. (*Cunard*)

Below right: The second Cunard queen, the 1,031-foot-long *Queen Elizabeth*, is shorter only than the 1,250-foot-tall Empire State Building. (*Cunard*)

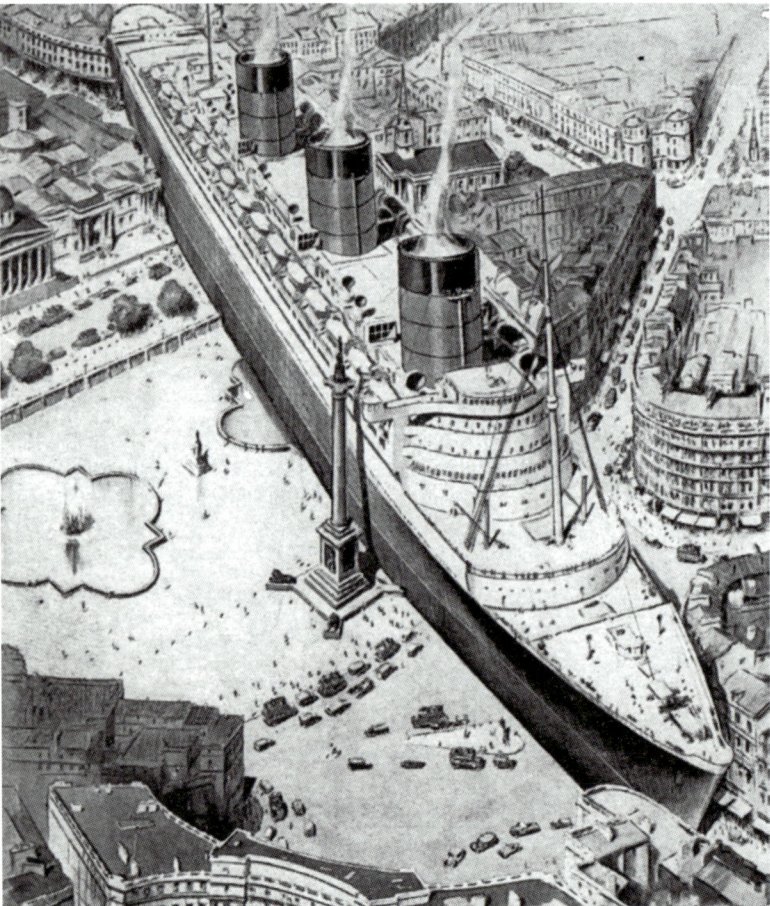

Both the *Queen Mary* (seen here arriving at New York in June 1945) and the *Queen Elizabeth* did heroic, highly important work as troop ships during the Second World War. They had been specially outfitted to carry as many as 15,000 soldier-passengers per crossing. (*Ernest Arroyo Collection*)

Wedged between the buildings of Manhattan's West Side, the *Queen Mary* departs in a gala send-off for the last time. The date is September 1967. (*Author's Collection*)

Twelve

THE GREAT RECORD BREAKER
The Empire State Building

Like the Chrysler, the Empire State Building was true 1930s modernism. The Empire State Building was over-the-top as well and very Art Deco. It was also a very practical building in some ways. The architects used the same paneling floor after floor and this was very economical. At first, the rooftop was flat and stopped at a point that was just about 3 feet taller than the Chrysler Building. The owners wanted a distinctive building, in fact the tallest yet. But what to do? A designer, John J Raskob, who had worked previously in upper management at General Motors, had no love for Walter Chrysler. Raskob and his company came up with an idea for a mooring tower at the very top of the Empire State Building. This pushed-up the height of the building and actually had an added purpose: a mooring mast for big trans-Atlantic Zeppelins. It could never work, of course. It was far too dangerous having a Zeppelin attached at 1,250 feet above the City. The wind and down drafts could easily have the likes of the 900-foot-long *Graf Zeppelin* pointing upwards by the tail.

It is very interesting to see that every one of the tallest buildings following the Singer in 1909 was built to top a rival. Metropolitan Life topped the Singer and then the Woolworth Building topped Metropolitan Life. And sometimes it was personal rivalries: William van Allen and his Chrysler Building wanted to top his former partner Craig Severance and his 40 Wall Street tower with a surprise last minute spire. And finally, Raskob topping the Chrysler with the last minute addition of the mooring tower on the Empire State Building.

Everyone knew it would not work, but it succeeded in making the Empire State the world's tallest for some four decades.

Albert Wilhelmi

As built, the 102-floor Empire State Building had a top height of 1,250 feet. The antenna, added in 1950, pushed the full height to 1,472 feet.

Deriving its name from the nickname for New York State, this beloved building is considered one of the greatest icons of New York City. Along with the Statue of Liberty, Rockefeller Center, and the Brooklyn Bridge, the building is also a great tourist symbol. When completed in May 1931, the price tag for the building was put at $40,948,900 (or $635,000,000 in 2015 dollars). Now owned by the Empire State Realty Trust, the building had a $550,000,000 renovation in 2010. Some $120,000,000 was spent to make the building more efficient and eco-friendly.

Built on the site of the original Waldorf-Astoria Hotel, the building was designed in just two weeks by William F. Lamb of the firm Shreve, Lamb & Harmon. The architects used plans from two other but smaller buildings, the Reynolds Building in Winston-Salem, North Carolina, and Cincinnati's Carew Tower. Design began from the top down and construction began on 17 March 1930. From the very start, the project involved 3,400 workers, many of them

The 102-floors of the Empire State Building are all but completed in this view from 1931. (*Author's Collection*)

European immigrants, but also hundreds of Mohawk Indians. Five workers died during the 410 days of construction.

Projected to take eighteen months to construct, progress was steady, and the building was finished in fifteen months. In all, the construction was a record an achievement; it was the world's first building to surpass 1,100 feet in height and was built in one year and forty-five days. The building was opened on 1 May 1931 in appropriately dramatic fashion; President Herbert Hoover switched-on the building's lights with the push of a button, although he did so from Washington, DC Ironically, the building's tower lights were first switched-on in November 1932 to signal the election of Franklin D. Roosevelt who defeated Herbert Hoover

The Empire State Building could not have been built at a less auspicious time. The Great Depression had set-in and the almost immediately figures were devastating. A year after the Great Depression began, investors had lost $40 billion and more than 6 million people were out of work, 5,000 banks failed and 32,000 businesses were bankrupt. In New York City, there were breadlines, people reduced to living in huts and near riots. Consequently, the new building had far fewer tenants than expected. It was soon dubbed the 'Empty State' Building. Rental problems were complicated further by the building's location, on 34th Street and Fifth Avenue. It was a considerable distance from Grand Central Station as well as Penn Station and the then newly built Port Authority Bus Terminal. The Chrysler Building, by comparison and across the street from Grand Central Station, was all but fully rented in 1931. The Empire State Building earned $2,000,000 in rents in 1931–32, the same amount taken in for its observation deck.

A patient photographer has captured a unique moment—summer lightning striking the tip of the antenna of the Empire State Building. (*Author's Collection*)

The building did not become profitable until well after the end of the Second World War, in 1950. It also changed hands at about the same time and, selling for $51,000,000, was then the highest price paid for a single structure.

The Empire State Building made headlines just weeks before the Japanese surrender and end of the Second World War. On a Saturday morning, 28 July 1945, a B-25 bomber crashed into the north side between the seventy-ninth and eightieth floors. Fourteen were killed and the resulting fire took forty minutes to extinguish. An elevator operator plunged seventy-five floors in a shaft that had survived the initial impact. A year later, in 1946, another plane nearly crashed into the building.

Expectedly, the building has impressive statistics, with 6,500 windows, seventy-three elevators, 1,000 tenants, and over 20,000 people who work in the building each day. Added facts include 70 miles of pipe, 2,500,000 feet of electrical wiring, and 9,000 faucets.

In the 1950s, the top of the building contained sets of searchlights that circled around the top and which could be seen for miles. In 1964, these were changed to floodlights on the upper floors and, by 1976, the colors changed to match holidays and special occasions. These included being green for St Patrick's Day, blue for the death of Frank Sinatra, and in tennis-ball yellow for the opening of the US Open Tennis tournament. In 2012, the upper floor lighting was changed to LED fixtures, using a computer-controlled system that has virtually limitless color configurations.

A morning in 1936: looking south from the top of the seventy-story RCA Building with the Empire State Building as the focal point. (*Der Scutt Collection*)

In 1983, for the fiftieth anniversary of the film *King Kong*, a 90-foot-tall inflatable King Kong was briefly placed on the building near the observation deck.

The Empire State Building remained the tallest man-made structure for twenty-three years before it was surpassed by the Griffin Television Tower in Oklahoma. One World Trade Center, the north tower, surpassed the height of the Empire State Building in 1972. There had been a short-lived plan in the early 1970s to dismantle the mooring tower and antenna and replace them with an additional eleven floors. After the attacks on 11 September 2001, the Empire State Building again became the tallest building in New York City. It was surpassed, however, by the new World Trade Center on 30 April 2012.

Limitless amounts of replicas have been made of the Empire State Building and these include a 7½-foot version made of 12,000 Lego bricks. A foot race from the ground floor to the observation deck has been held annually since 1978. Contestants include runners as well as climbers, and also skyscraper enthusiasts. The race covers a distance of 1,050 feet and takes in 1,576 steps. The record time, accomplished in 2003, is nine minutes and thirty-three seconds.

Far left: The Empire State Building had a fiftieth celebration with special laser lighting in May 1981. (*Author's Collection*)

Near left: Skilled workmen affix the 222-foot-tall antenna atop the Empire State Building in 1950. (*Der Scutt Collection*)

Low-lying clouds evocatively surround five midtown towers: 10 East 40th Street, 500 Fifth Avenue, New York Life, Metropolitan Life, and the Empire State. (*Der Scutt Collection*)

Thirteen

LAST OF A MARITIME BREED
United States, France, Queen Elizabeth 2, and Queen Mary 2

ALMOST SUDDENLY, ON AN OTHERWISE flawless late summer morning, we realized that the era of the great Atlantic ocean liner was over. The airlines had won and the liners, losing passengers and their income, were cast into a new role—floating dinosaurs. That day, 22 September 1967, the illustrious *Queen Mary* departed from New York for the last time, 1,000 crossings in her wake and a last complement of mostly loyalist and sentimental passengers aboard. The *Queen Elizabeth*, her fleet mate and other half of the great Cunard *Queens*, would follow into retirement thirteen months later.

The trans-Atlantic liner trade boomed for a full decade following the end of the Second World War, from the late '40s to the late '50s. New ships were built, older, pre-war ones restored, and the 'ocean liner sweepstakes', for bigger and faster vessels, resumed. Ships like the *Queens* and *Ile de France* were restored to their luxurious selves after strenuous war service and all while the pre-war *Europa* reappeared by as the French *Liberte*. For brand-new ships, it was rather ironic that the Americans produced the most important liner of its time. Previously, US-flag ship owners seemed content with medium-sized and even secondhand liners, but the new liner was the exceptional *United States*, a 53,300-tonner commissioned in July 1952 and sparked by two considerations—the potential for showing the flag and making a profit on the Atlantic, but (and perhaps more importantly) her use as a 15,000 to 18,000-capacity troop ship in case of war. It was said she could be converted in forty-eight hours and,

to some critics, that the 990-foot-long liner was really 'a troopship disguised as a passenger liner'. Washington would control her design, incorporate many ideas of its own (mostly military) and, in the end, pay for 70 percent of her whopping $78-million cost. The 1,928-passenger ship had to be exceptionally safe and have amazing speed. On her trials, she reached an amazing 43 knots and then captured the Blue Riband from the *Queen Mary* with crossings of over 38 knots. She was, in fact, the last liner to hold the Blue Riband. No other liner would be faster—there would be no need.

In October 1958, the first commercial jets flew the Atlantic. It was now hours rather than days. Almost immediately, it was all over for the traditional liners. Within five years, the airlines captured 98 percent of all travelers. Winter crossings all but disappeared and even those once crowded summer voyages dwindled steadily. 'You could be in the main lounge and sitting almost alone at tea time. Your only company was the stewards and the violinists', recalled one longtime Cunard Line loyalist.

However, the old order died slowly; commissioned in 1962, the 66,348-gross-ton *France* was the very last super liner to be built almost solely for North Atlantic crossings. She was 1,035 feet in length, the longest liner yet built. Heavily underwritten by the French government, she endured for only twelve years, supported by loyalist travelers and her reputation for having the finest kitchens on all the seas. 'You could never ever diet onboard the *France*', said one longtime Atlantic traveler.

Clockwise from above left:

Outbound, the *Queen Elizabeth 2* passes Lower Manhattan and the iconic Twin Towers. (*Cunard*)

Modern age: Cunard's three queens—*Queen Elizabeth* (top left), *Queen Victoria*, and just arriving, the 1,132-foot-long *Queen Mary 2* in a view at Southampton, England, dated May 2014. (*Cunard*)

Meeting of the ages: the stately *Queen Mary* of 1936 meets the *Queen Mary 2* of 2004 at Long Beach, California. The date is February 2006. (*Cunard*)

The new, 2010-built *Queen Elizabeth* passes a gleaming Manhattan skyline while outbound on a 100-night cruise around the world in January 2011. (*Cunard*)

The three Cunard queens departing in formation in January 2011—*Queen Elizabeth* (left), *Queen Victoria*, and *Queen Mary 2*. (*Cunard*)

Maiden arrival: the brilliant *United States*, the fastest liner of all time, arrives in New York harbor the first time in June 1952. (*United States Lines*)

The 1,035-foot-long *France*—the world's longest liner—passes the Lower Manhattan skyline in this view dated 1962. (*French Line*)

Three years after the *France*, the Italians created not one but two big liners, the 45,900-ton *Michelangelo* and *Raffaello*. Cunard could not be left out and so, in 1969, added the 65,800-ton *Queen Elizabeth 2*. Perhaps most sensible of all, this 2,005-passenger ship had a practical approach—six months on crossings and the other six in lucrative, leisure cruising. Thought at first to be a less than sound proposition, the 963-foot-long *QE2* went on to be the most successful Atlantic liner of all time. She endured at Cunard for thirty-nine years, steamed more miles, traveled to more ports, and made more money than any big liner in history. Retired in late 2008, she even beat the scrap merchants and instead was sold to Dubai interests (for a whopping $100 million) for use as a floating residence, museum and entertainment complex.

The Atlantic sealanes were quite empty by the mid-'70s; the *United States* was retired in 1969, the *France* decommissioned five years later, and then the *Michelangelo* and *Raffaello* made their final trips in 1975. Only the *QE2* was left and thought by many to be the last big liner. In 1998, however, when Miami-based Carnival Corporation, the biggest and richest cruise operator in the world, bought Cunard (for $600 million), they quickly invested an additional $800 million to build the 151,000-ton, 2,600-passenger *Queen Mary 2*, the largest Atlantic super ship ever and said to be the 'last true ocean liner'. Like the *QE2*, she would divide her working year—half in crossings, half in cruises. Business and maritime nostalgia thrived. In 2014, the 1,132-foot-long *Queen Mary 2* celebrated her first decade of highly successful service and at the same time, the Cunard flagship, once the largest at sea, dropped to sixth place. Bigger and bigger cruise ships were being built—and more are planned for the future.

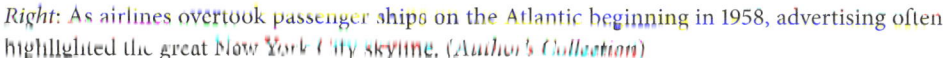

Above: Inbound, the *Norway*—the restyled former *France*—passes the World Trade Center. This scene dates from 5 September 2001. (*William Donall/Robert O'Brien*)

Right: As airlines overtook passenger ships on the Atlantic beginning in 1958, advertising often highlighted the great New York City skyline. (*Author's Collection*)

Fourteen

TWINS ABOVE THE HUDSON
The World Trade Center

Beginning in 1979 and for several years thereafter, the author worked on the eighty-sixth floor of 1 World Trade Center, the north tower; it was a unique experience. The views were, of course, spectacular, the building sometimes 'moaned and creaked' (like a ship at sea) in high winds and, within the fire stairs, there was sometimes an ethereal chorus of 'whistling,' again the winds. Especially in winter, we were sometimes shrouded in gray clouds, and then there were no views—just that dullest of colors. Working in the towers and on a high floor you felt special, quite different, even in skyscraper-crowded New York City.

> I feel there was a similarity between the French liner *France* [1962] and the World Trade Center [1973]. Myself, I was shocked by the interiors of the *France*. They were cold, indifferent, even cheap. The same was true with the World Trade Center. They lacked the greater style, the high quality that they should have had. But unlike the *France*, the World Trade Center was also unattractive on the outside. They were too big, dull, unimaginative from almost any angle.
>
> Albert Wilhelmi

The Twin Towers, as they were often dubbed, opened on 4 April 1973. At the time, 1 World Trade Center—the north tower—was 1,368 feet in height and the tallest building in the world. Nearby, but unnoticeable to the human eye, 2 World Trade Center was in fact 6 feet shorter, measuring 1,362 feet. A 360-foot-tall antenna was added to the north tower in 1978. Along with six other buildings in the World Trade Center complex, built between 1975 and 1985, the total construction cost was placed at $400,000,000 (or $2,400,000,000 in 2015 dollars).

Originally planned as one tower of ninety floors and placed along the East River side of Lower Manhattan, the project was rethought and redone to include not only the two larger towers but in a position along the Hudson River. To stir growth in Lower Manhattan, the project was suggested by David Rockefeller, then chairman of Chase Manhattan Bank and which had its headquarters nearby. The actual idea of a building for world trade dated back to the Second World War, in 1943, then progressed slowly and finally was put on hold in 1949. It had renewed interest and so planning restarted in the late 1950s. Eventually, the area known as Radio Row—so named for the countless, often small shops selling used radio and electronics equipment—was selected. The Port Authority of New York & New Jersey, the bi-state governmental agency owning and overseeing bridges, tunnels, transportation, airports, and marine terminals, was selected to be placed in charge of the World Trade Center project. Much of Radio Row was acquired in 1964, the owners bought out for $3,000 each and then demolition followed in 1965–66.

Right: Imposing: the 110-floor World Trade Center towers stand high above the Lower Manhattan skyline. The sixty-story Woolworth Building is on the far left. (*Albert Wilhelmi Collection*)

Below: A void in the Lower Manhattan skyline as seen in this view from the cruise ship *Crystal Symphony* in a photo dated September 2003. (*Author's Collection*)

Minoru Yamasaki was selected as the lead architect and, in fact, originally planned two eighty-story towers. The Port Authority's request for as much as 10,000,000 square feet of office space pushed the plan to 110 floors for each tower, however. Among the difficulties faced by Yamasaki were too many space-consuming elevator banks in such tall buildings. Consequently, a new system was invented—two 'sky lobbies' (on the forty-forth and seventy-eighth floors) were created and where people could switch from a high-capacity to a local elevator. The idea was said to have been inspired by the New York City subway system. Altogether, the World Trade Center had ninety-five express and local elevators. Yamasaki's plans also called for narrow-width windows (18 inches wide), which reflected not only his own fear of heights, but the general desire to make occupants feel more secure, even safe. Yamasaki also decided to sheath the buildings in a silvery aluminum alloy.

Groundbreaking for construction was held on 5 August 1966. Actual construction on the north tower began in August 1968, with the south tower's construction commencing in January 1969. The topping-out of 1 World Trade Center (the north tower) took place in December 1970 and 2 World Trade Center in the following July. The price for the towers alone was fixed at $900 million.

The towers were not especially well-received at first, and they were only 50 percent occupied. In a critique in the *New York Times,* it was suggested that the two buildings might be better used by being pushed over and made into

The north tower of the World Trade Center under construction in 1970. (*Moran Towing and Transportation Co.*)

the two biggest tunnels to and from New Jersey. An architectural journal, equally less enthused about the design and appearance of the buildings, described them as 'little more than glass and metal filing cabinets.' Another critique described them as 'purposeless giantism.'

Within time, however, the towers grew in popularity and success, and (like the Empire State Building, Chrysler Building and Statue of Liberty) became structural symbols of New York City. By the 1990s, 50,000 people were working in them and another 200,000 passed through daily as visitors. On its 16-acre site with five smaller buildings, the World Trade Center even had its own zip code (10048). There was an observation deck on the south tower and a swank restaurant, Windows on the World, atop the north tower. Along with shops, restaurants and links to subways, one of the world's largest gold depositories was stored well beneath the towers. The World Trade Center was privatized in 2001 and was leased to a private real estate firm.

The north tower was bombed in an Islamist terrorist attack on 26 February 1993, causing underground damages, killing six people, and causing the 50,000 occupants to evacuate. Some were forced to walk down darkened stairwells in difficult evacuations that took as long as two hours.

Eighteen years later, on 11 September 2001, the World Trade Center was destroyed. Two hijacked airliners crashed into the towers, causing them to burn and then collapse, killing 2,606 people. One firm, Cantor Fitzgerald, located on 101st-105th floors of the north tower, lost 658 employees.

After the last fires were extinguished or burned out, the clean-up process began and continued round-the-clock; clean-up was officially completed in eight months, by 30 May 2002. Almost immediately, that November, plans for renewal and rebuilding began and soon included a memorial park, museum, other buildings, and the construction of the 1,776-foot-tall Freedom Tower, later renamed 1 World Trade Center.

Seen the from the top deck of the inbound P&O cruise ship *Victoria*, the World Trade Center on the morning of 7 September 2001. (*Harley Crossley*)

Fifteen

FLOATING RESORTS IN THE SUN
The Oasis of the Seas and Allure of the Seas

I JUST COULDN'T RESIST—I HAD TO make a voyage aboard the *Allure of the Seas*, then the world's largest passenger ship ever. It was the winter of 2011 and the ship was barely two months old. On a sunny Sunday afternoon, we boarded the 225,000-ton, 6,400-passenger *Allure of the Seas*, the biggest ocean liner ever built. She's even a tad bigger (just 2 inches actually) than her otherwise twin sister, the *Oasis of the Seas*. So, she made my record book—she is my very first super-duper mega-liner. The mind boggled, my eyes widened, my imagination deeply tweaked. The 1,187-foot-long *Allure* (that's some 75,000 tons and 50 feet longer than another giant liner, the 151,000-ton *Queen Mary 2*) and a towering 213 feet high is every inch the 'floating vacation resort'. Yes, a ship that is more—much more—than just another 'floating hotel'. I was completely dazzled. For sure, she could have been named 'Colossus of the Seas'.

I was not alone in being over-impressed; a friend from Florida, who just happened to be aboard the same ship, smilingly commented, 'This ship is just magical! It is like another world, a world that is creative and beautiful, but also fantasy-like, even child-like. It is a ship where dreams come true. It is the most remarkable creation ever to sail the seas. And you never, ever feel that there are 6,000 other passengers onboard'.

It was a great day for cruising. On that Sunday, no less than nine liners were berthed together in Port Everglades. The group included the likes of the *Queen Elizabeth*, *Queen Victoria*, *Celebrity Solstice*, *MSC Poesia*, and two Holland America ships among them. It was

estimated that well over 20,000 passengers had arrived that morning and all had departed long before the south Florida sun set in early evening. Port Everglades/Fort Lauderdale had become the biggest, busiest cruise port anywhere on the planet and their all-time record of handling a dozen cruise ships at once still holds.

At the port, and just after lunch, we boarded the immense *Allure* and along with some 6,100 other passengers bound for a week of floating entertainment coupled with the Caribbean sun and warmth. A new, mega-cruise terminal befits the ship and the boarding process takes just a few minutes, with smiles everywhere. We are whisked through security, checked-in with split-second speed and then crossed a glass-tube gangway and boarded this behemoth of the seas.

Like some skyscraper, we were quickly off to our cabin up on Deck 12 (out of the ship's soaring seventeen decks and said to be equal to a twenty-story building on shore). Beginning with our Indonesian cabin steward, it was all friendly smiles and easy chatter, and those much-needed, helpful directions from step one. Immediately, one senses that the *Allure of the Seas* is not only the biggest liner afloat, but the friendliest. Pure, absolute charm from Royal Caribbean International, the Miami-based owners of the ship, who themselves are owned by super-rich Norwegian ship owners (the Wilhelmsen Lines), and Chicago-based hoteliers (the Pritzker family and their Hyatt Regency chain). In total, there's a staggering 2,384 crew onboard from no less than eighty nations.

The public areas are meant to be exciting, and they often are. They are colorfully imaginative feasts to the eye and great applause should be given to the designers and interior decorators—it is Disneyland coupled with Disney World coupled with Sea World and all glossed over by the genius of, say, a dozen Las Vegas hotels. One lady from Minnesota said, 'I don't know which way to look next. Everything is so beautiful, so interesting, just so stunning!' A cruise-only travel agent from Florida added, 'I've never seen people more excited about a ship!'

All aboard! At embarkation (and based on online preferences made months before), the main ingredients of our evening schedules are prepared, organized, and thoughtfully printed out—it becomes our guide. On the very first night, it was 'My Time Dining' (with unassigned tables in the huge, three-deck high main restaurant, but candied by more of that exceptionally friendly Royal Caribbean service) at 5.45 p.m. to 7.45 p.m. and then, walking a 'mile or two or three' to the forward-placed Amber Theater (yes, more sheer enormity with 2,200 seats) for a ninety-minute production of *Chicago*.

Decorative originality, even splendor. In between dinner and the show, we strolled the Royal Promenade, a long, horizontal promenade area with shops, bars, clubs, yet more eateries, and added touches like the gourmet Cupcake Cupboard (there's even cupcake-themed jewelry and handbags) and then to the Boardwalk (an amusement park with Johnny Rockets, ice cream and hot dog bars, a full merry-go-round, and another massive, eye-popping amenity—the 750-seat, open-air Aqua Theater, located at the very stern of this most unique 'floating resort'). There's also jazz and comedy clubs, a huge disco, art gallery, photo studio, make-your-own-stuffed-animal shop, conference room, library, jogging track, internet center, pizzeria, complete English pub (with dark and rich wooded interiors), champagne bar, Solera cosmetics emporium, donut and candy shops, Mexican cantina, ice cream parlor, and the very first Starbucks to hit the high seas. You can be certified in scuba diving, take ice-skating classes, play basketball or miniature golf, join scrapbook-making seminars, or enter the Lady Gaga Dress-Up contest.

The ship, which cost $1.5 billion to create, was built at the huge STX Europe Shipyard at Turku in Finland. The *Allure*'s a whopping 208 feet wide (almost like one of those monster US Navy aircraft carriers), draws 30 feet of water, can speed along at a very respectable 22 knots and has those soaring seventeen passenger decks. Then there are twenty-one restaurants and ten hot tubs, and it takes fifteen to twenty minutes to walk completely around the largest top deck. With great ease and steady comfort, there are twenty-four passenger elevators to cater to a maximum of 6,318 passengers, comfortably housed in no less than 2,706 suites and staterooms. The suites include duplex lofts, something of a novelty at sea, and sell (at least in a brochure rate) for $14,000 per week for two. However, the average daily per person rate aboard the *Allure* is a much more affordable $218.

The 6,400-passenger *Allure of the Seas* in the Caribbean in January 2011. (*Author's Collection*)

Slightly worrying to the companies behind the ships, both the *Oasis* and *Allure* came into service at an undeniably bad time; this was during the international recession that began in the fall of 2008, and which had been cruel in ways. Within a year, Royal Caribbean's sales hit only $1.8 billion, a 14 percent decrease in twelve months, but there was some sunshine, even if a bit hazy. Some four dozen new cruise ships came on or are coming on line even in these tough times. Through massive, across-the-board discounting, the US cruise industry had a record 102 percent occupancy in 2010 and while air-sea cruises in Europe were, quite frankly, booming. In Europe itself, both the British and German cruise markets were rising by leaps and bounds—there was some hope for cruise liners.

Our first day at sea was just the start of busy days and busy nights. 'The ship's daily program is more like a magazine,' noted one fellow passenger. 'There is so much to read, to absorb, so much to do.' We start the day with a grand gala parade of singers and dancers of DreamWorks characters—yes, *Shrek* was there and the full cast too. There were banners and balloons, knights on horses, a full Chinese brigade and (dangling from a cable high above) the glistening good fairy, in silvery gown and glittering crown and scepter.

By night, we were 'booked,' according to our personalized cruiser printout, to see the hour-long *Ice Games*; with soft, ever-changing lights and varied music from Puccini to Michael Jackson to Brazilian samba, this visually-skillful show is cleverly themed to a giant Monopoly game and, as the foam-filled 'big dice' roll, the themes change. Even a complete castle moves out onto the rink. Champion guest skaters all the way from Moscow are the cherries on the cake tonight. Afterward, it was the captain's 'Welcome Aboard' blast, held in the vast promenade and, as expected, with a large assembled crowd. The captain waves, a few (by personal preference actually) shake his hand, as a band up on a perch fills the place with the classic sound of 1960s Burt Bacharach. Just about everyone was in high form—dressy, glittery, a few real show-stoppers. There are some great gowns, some feathers and even a few fur wraps, Japanese kimonos and Scottish kilts, a group of Nigerian ladies in colorful robes, and a heavily bemedaled US Army officer.

Cold courage—one of the Zipline onboard attendants said, 'We had an eighty-seven-year-old man doing it just last week.' Well, with watch off, pockets emptied, and tight shoes in place, I was strapped in

The 225,000-ton *Allure of the Seas* and the 142,000-ton *Voyager of the Seas* emphasizes the differences in cruise ship size within eleven years (1999–2010).

(and very tightly) and 'swung' across the aft end of the ship, eighteen stories above the waterline. At that very last minute, as you step off the edge of the steel platform, you look downward and suddenly you are much like, say, a window-washer high atop the Empire State Building. Off I went—straight across. Then the finish—the quick, quite abrupt, stop-in-your-own-tracks landing. A welcome from a competent and welcoming attendant at the opposite end—bodily perfection.

On one night and just before our late dinner, we attended *OceanAria*, the ship's grandiose aqua show, staged of course, quite appropriately, in the open-air Aqua Theatre at the stern. It was purely spectacular—high precision, cascading fountains and colorful water sprays, rousing music, elaborate costuming, and even sprinkles of comedy. Mostly, it was all a grand showing, a tribute in fact, to sheer physical perfection. The bodies of the entire aquatic team, mostly male, reflected human architecture—the leanest, most finely developed form in what seems to be 8½-foot-tall frames, well detailed muscles, the broadest of shoulders, the sturdiest and firmest of legs, that most impressive ability to bend, twist, contort. Two super-solid Ukrainians stood out, both being more like industrial machinery than mere mortals, with their seemingly limitless lifting skills.

Mega-success—Royal Caribbean International remains the second largest cruise operator in the world with, combining their other divisions, then numbering some forty-five ships and so second only to the colossal Carnival Group, with a worldwide fleet of some ninety liners. These are all sensibly well divided, of course; Royal Caribbean also owns successful, well-rated Celebrity Cruises and then has separate British, German, and Spanish cruise subsidiaries. Specifically, the Royal Caribbean fleet has twenty-two cruise ships under its direct banner or something in the way of 80,000 beds a week to fill on worldwide cruises (and which includes departure ports such as New York City, Southampton, Barcelona, Dubai, Sydney, Osaka, and Buenos Aires, to name a few).

A stroll in the ship's Central Park was refreshing and certainly relaxing, especially considering that there was 6,000-plus passengers onboard. The recreated Central Park, filled with 'real' trees and greenery, included electronic bird and even cricket sounds. Altogether, there are some 12,000 plants tended by a full-time onboard horticulturist. Lots of the plants are labeled and there's also daily garden tours. There's also benches, soft chairs, and well-cushioned easy chairs along the way. Great vines and strands of ivy climb upwards along the inner decks and are suitably lighted by night. In fact, the only thing better than the serenity of the park by day was the sheer tranquility of it by night—a never-crowded refuge of deep relaxation and high reflection at sea.

The highest respect and praises go to Royal Caribbean's gigantic *Allure of the Seas*, which is highly recommended to all. She was, to us, a smash hit, something totally different and refreshing in cruising. She and her sister ship are of course in a class of their own.

'It's hard to think of a word to best sum up the *Allure of the Seas*,' penned British cruise writer Jeremy Dickinson. 'So I am going to borrow the one Royal Caribbean itself uses. "Wow!" It's short, sweet, to the point, and says it all!'

Sixteen

RENEWAL AND REBIRTH
The 'New' World Trade Center

While the *Queen Mary 2* is called the last of the great liners, she is also the last true 'ocean liner'. She is also the biggest Atlantic liner ever created. The new World Trade Center is similar. The Tower—the tallest building in the Western Hemisphere—is very similar. The *Queen Mary 2* and the new World Trade Center are, I feel, both beautiful and both elegant and unique.

Albert Wilhelmi

AFTER A SERIES OF COMPETITIONS and voting processes, plans for the new World Trade Center were finally approved. Four-and-a-half years after the attack and destruction of the original towers, the final removal work and first survey work began on 13 March 2006. Ground was broken for the Freedom Tower some five weeks later, on 27 April. Gradually rising above the Lower Manhattan skyline, the building reached fifty-two floors on 11 September 2011 and was topped-off on 10 May 2013, receiving its first commercial tenants in the fall of 2014. At 1,776 feet, the height is a deliberate reference to the year of American Independence.

Costing $3.9 billion, the new building has ninety-four floors, but—with the very top floor below the roof being counted—the final count is 105 floors. Counting the 408-foot spire, the World Trade Center ranked, in early 2015, as the fourth tallest building in the world and, as mentioned, the tallest in the Western Hemisphere.

While very tall buildings are planned or being built throughout the world and some in New York City itself, the World Trade Center will remain special—a great symbol. It is a symbol of progress, with buildings still soaring and to new and greater heights. On the high seas, there will be a continuation of even larger ships being built. The age of sailing and soaring goes on.

The World Trade Center under construction in 2013. (*Author's Collection*)

BIBLIOGRAPHY

Berenholtz, R., *New York Deco*, (Welcome Books, 2005)

Braynard, F. O., and Miller, W. H., *Fifty Famous Liners*, (Patrick Stephens Ltd, 1982)

De Kerbrech, R. P., and Williams, D. L., *Cunard White Star Liners of the 1930s*, (Conway Maritime Press Ltd, 1988)

Miller, W. H., *Famous Ocean Liners*, (Patrick Stephens Ltd, 1987)

Miller, W. H., *Ocean Liners: Travel on the Open Seas*, (Mallard Press, 1990)

Miller, W. H., *Pictorial Encyclopedia of Ocean Liners 1860–1994*, (Dover Publications Inc., 1995)

Miller, W. H., *The Last Atlantic Liners*, (Conway Maritime Press Ltd, 1985)

Morton, A., *Theirs is the Kingdom*, (Summit Books, 1989)

The World Trade Center in winter 2015. (*Author's Collection*)